C000173253

MEDITERRANEO EDITIONS

Kos

THE ISLAND & THE CITY

Text by
STELLA KALOGERAKI
Archaeologist

Photographs
STELLA KALOGERAKI - GEORGE MARKOULAKIS

Layout
VANGELIS PAPIOMYTOGLOU

DTP
NATASSA ANTONAKI

Translation
JILL PITTINGER

Copyright 2005
MEDITERRANEO EDITIONS
Tel. +3028310 21590, Fax: +3028310 21591

www.mediterraneo.gr

ISBN: 960-8227-50-X

KOS

THE ISLAND & THE CITY

C O N T E N T S

4

CONTENTS

Geography – Geomorphology

Like the Cyclades in the distant past the island group of the Dodecanese, which includes Kos, constituted part of Aegaea, a unified continental landmass which covered the whole area from Thrace to the south of Crete, and from the Ionian Sea to Asia Minor. Later tectonic movements brought about the breakup of this landmass which resulted in the formation of the Aegean Sea and the islands. The geomorphology of Kos is of such complexity that, from as early as the 19th century onwards, it drew the attention of many researchers whose particular areas of interest were its geology, volcanic genesis, palaeontology, and fossils. The geomorphology and geographical configuration of Kos, which is part of the "island volcanic arc of the south-eastern Aegean", have been decisively influenced by the activity of the Eurasian and African tectonic plates. Together with Yiali and Nisyros, Kos is considered to constitute one of the more typical parts of the volcanic arc of the southern Aegean, with rocks formed by the gradual extrusion of lava. Accordingly, the volcanic activity on Kos and Nisyros is limited and manifests itself only through secondary phenomena, such as thermal springs.

PATMOS

LEROS

KALIMNOS

KOS

NISYROS

SIMI

ASTIPALEA

TILOS

CHALKI

RHODES

KARPATHOS

KASOS

*The little island of 'Kastri'
in the Bay of Kefalos.*

MYTHOLOGY

Gigantomachy (the battle of the giants). Relief from the frieze of the Temple of Zeus at Pergamon. 180 BC.

A large number of important events in Greek mythology are associated with Kos. One of these is the famous **Gigantomachy**, a terrible conflict between the giants - who were the sons of Uranos and Gaia – and the gods of Olympos; both sides sought power over the world. The gods were the victors and put the giants to flight; some of them – namely Phoibos, Koios and Kynnos - fled to Kos and it is said that the name of 'Kynnis' that was given to the island derived from the latter. The myth surrounding the giant Polybotes is of particular interest; it relates that after the victory of the gods, Poseidon pursued the giant, cut off a piece of Kos with his trident and squashed him with it. It is said that Nisyros, a small neighbouring island, was thus formed, covering Polybotes for eternity. Possibly, this myth may echo the belief that Nisyros, in the very distant past, was joined to Kos. Many of the other heroes

The names of the island

The island, which in mythology is closely connected with the savage war between the Giants and the Titans, acquired a number of names such as *Kynnis* , after the Titan Kynnos, *Meropis* after the mythological king Merops, *Karis* from the Kares or from the shape of the island, which is that of a 'garida' (Class. Greek 'karida', meaning a type of shellfish), *Nymphaia* after the Nymphs, and ' *Island of the Blest*', because of the prosperity and comfortable life of its inhabitants. Its name today, according to researchers, derives either from Koos, the daughter of the mythical king Triops or Merops, or from the word 'kos' which means 'crab'; the latter is often depicted on its ancient coinage. The medieval name of the island, given to it by the Knights of St. John, was *Langos*, and later it was called *Neratzia*, because of the great number of citrus trees which were to be found there. Later, the Turks called Kos 'Stankiöy', which probably originated from the Greek 'stin Ko', meaning 'on/to Kos'.

Poseidon pursued the giant Polybotes and crushed him with a piece of land which he cut from Kos with his trident. Thereafter, this was said to have formed the island of Nisyros.

Herakles killed the sea-monster and saved Hesione.

and demigods of Greek mythology are connected with the island. **Herakles**, the son of Zeus, king of the gods, and the mortal Alcmene, lived under the shadow of the hatred and threats of Hera who had been deceived by her husband. When the hero was married, Hera implanted a madness in him and drove him to kill his wife, Megara, and his children. As soon as Herakles realized his mistake, he fled to the oracle at Delphi to ask what he was to do in atonement; the oracle counselled him to go and serve Eurystheus, king of Tiryns. When Herakles arrived there, the king commanded him to accomplish twelve dangerous missions, with the intention of destroying him. When the hero, with unexpected success, had carried out the twelve labours, the insatiable and obstinate Eurystheus forced him to carry out a series of lesser tasks, one of which was a mission to Troy to save the royal princess Hesione. Laomedon, son of Troas, was king of Troy; he had provoked the anger of Poseidon through not having given thanks to the god when he had built the walls of the city. To punish him, the god had sent a monster which emerged from the sea and devastated everything in the vicinity. In panic, Laomedon had appealed to the oracle at Delphi, from which he learned how this evil might be stopped – he was to sacrifice his daughter, Hesione. The unhappy king had then promised that whoever killed the monster would take as a reward the horses which Zeus himself had given to his father. Although Herakles succeeded in killing the terrible monster and saving Hesione from sacrifice, Laomedon did not keep his promise. Full of anger and with the help of a few brave warriors, Herakles organized an expedition to Troy where he killed the king and laid waste to the city. He then

Mountainous Pyli. The naturally fortified locality in the inland region of Kos, where Herakles sought refuge.

started his journey back with six ships full of booty; however, a terrible storm sent by Hera, his eternal enemy, sank five of them. So, with one ship and only a few of his comrades, Herakles managed to reached Kos and land on the peninsula which is today known as Gourniates. Advancing inland, he and the comrades met Antagoras, a local shepherd who was keeping watch over his flock of sheep. Exhausted and starving, they asked the shepherd for one of his sheep so that they might have something to eat, but Antagoras refused.

Herakles attacked him and a battle flared immediately between the comrades and the inhabitants of the island, who had come to the assistance of the shepherd. When the hero managed to escape, he hid in the house of a woman from Thrace who helped him to disguise himself with her clothes and flee to mountainous Pyli, a fortified location in the middle of Kos, which from that time onwards was named "Phyxa", deriving from the word meaning 'flight' in Greek. The comrades did likewise; the Phyxiotes, an hospitable folk, welcomed the strangers and considering

the behaviour of the Antimahites unacceptable, helped Herakles to declare war on their king, Eurypylos. The hero not only managed to win the struggle but also to kill Eurypylos, even though he was the son of Poseidon. Thus the inhabitants of Antimahia were forced to stop the war, to declare Halkon, the son of Eurypylos, their king, and to give Halkiopi, the sister of Halkon, to Herakles as a wife. The son of Halkiopi was Thessalos, the subsequent king of Kos and Nisyros. The sons of the latter, according to Apollodorus, took part in the Trojan War with thirty ships.

The city of the Koans was formerly called Astypalaia and its inhabitants lived in another place which was probably also near the sea. Later, after some revolt, they moved to the current site, near to the Skandario Peninsula, and changed the name of the city to 'Kos', just as the whole island was named. Today the city is not large, but it is well laid-out and presents a pleasing sight to anyone who approaches the harbour from the sea. The size of the island is around 5,050 stades. There are fruit-bearing trees everywhere but, as in the case of Chios and Lesbos, the island is particularly known for its wine. In the south, near the ancient city of Alasarna, there is a peninsula from which Nisyros is only 60 stades distant. In the west there is Drekanon and a village named Stomalimni. Drekanon is about 200 stades from the city… In the suburbs there is the Asklepeion, a temple of huge fame, filled with innumerable dedicatory offerings, amongst which is the portrait of Antigonos by Apelles. 'Aphrodite Emerging from the Waves' was to be found there, before she was removed to Rome near the Divine Caesar, as an offering by Augustus who presented this representation of the founder of their line to his father. It is said, however, that the Koans received in exchange an exception from taxes which had been levied, to the tune of 100 talents. Furthermore, it is said that Hippocrates practised dietetics in the sanatorium which was located in this area. Thus he achieved renown, as did the doctor Simos, and in the same period Philetas, as a poet and critic. And then there was Aristonas, the pupil and heir of the Peripatetic School, and Theomnistos, the famous harpist and political opponent of Nikias.
Strabo, Geography

HISTORY

Prehistoric, Archaic and Classical periods

Due to its geographical location very near to the coast of Asia Minor, and also by reason of its geomorphology with extensive areas suited to cultivation, it was natural that from a very early time Kos would play an important role in the developments and events which took place in the Aegean. As is witnessed by the finds from the **Cave of Aspri Petra** in the south-west of the island, brought to light by the excavations of the Italian archaeologist Doro Levi in 1922, Kos was already inhabited during the late Neolithic period. At other places, mainly in the eastern part of the island, such as

The Italian archaeologist Doro Levi, excavator of the cave of Aspri Petra

Part of an archaic pediment with a helix. Archaeological Museum of Kos.

the location called **Troulli** (3 kms from the city of Kos), Akloupi, Tsilibiri and elsewhere, traces of habitation during the later Neolithic and early Bronze Age have also been discerned. Flakes of obsidian which originated from the

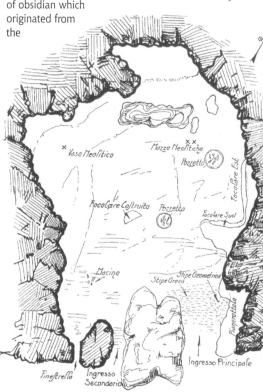

View of the cave of Aspri Petra. Sketch by the archaeologist Doro Levi.

nearby island of Yiali and obsidian tools from Melos have been found at Neolithic sites on Kos. This indicates that the obsidian of Yiali, although it was used for certain specific purposes, never

managed to supersede the famous Melian obsidian. Nevertheless, the Neolithic inhabitants of Kos colonized Yiali both periodically and seasonally; their motivation, if it was not the acquisition of obsidian, was certainly to bring back timber, since there were many

forests there which provided wood for boat building. Very little can be assumed in the case of the Early Bronze Age, even though it is certain that Kos in some way participated in the trade and traffic along the eastern Mediterranean - northern Aegean sea route. This is demonstrated with greater clarity during the Middle and Late Bronze Ages, where habitation is evidenced in the area of the modern city of Kos. According to some philological sources, the first habitation of the island was by the Pelasgians, the Karians and the Leleges. Some sources assign it to the 3rd millennium BC, which corresponds to the Early Bronze Age. Unfortunately, since it is very difficult to identify the people envisaged in the philological sources with those whose existence has been revealed by archaeologists' spades and pickaxes, the Pelasgians, the Karians and the Leleges will probably remain in our minds as mythical peoples. The supposed colonization of the island by the Phoenicians in the mid-2nd millennium should probably also be consigned to the same mythical sphere, since archaeological finds do not provide any conclusive evidence. According to Homer, Kos participated in the Trojan War with thirty ships and immediately after the fall of Troy, the Asklepiades (sons of Asklepios) came to the island and introduced the worship of Asklepios as the deliverer from

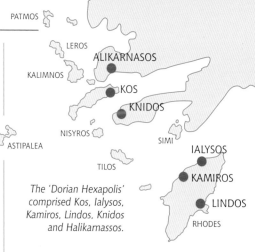

The 'Dorian Hexapolis' comprised Kos, Ialysos, Kamiros, Lindos, Knidos and Halikarnassos.

disease. Where the later descent into Greece of the Dorians in the 11th century (categorically mentioned in the historical reports) is concerned, the possibility cannot be excluded that it refers to peoples who came down from the mountainous areas to the lowland regions of Greece after the collapse of the Mycenaean system. Nevertheless, in accordance with tradition, at some point in time in the mid-11th century Dorian colonists arrived in Kos from the Argolid area of the Peloponnese. Herodotus states specifically that the colonists came from Dorian Epidauros. The archaeologist's spade confirmed this theory when it uncovered a Protogeometric cemetery which produced finds and evidence of the practice of funerary customs greatly resembling those of the Argolid in the corresponding period.

It is certain that the colonization of the 11th century BC brought about great improvement on the island at every level; this is more clearly seen in the subsequent archaic period, when Kos developed into a great economic power. Its importance was shown by its participation around 700 BC in the so-called 'Dorian Hexapolis', an economic, political and religious alliance which had as its headquarters the Sanctuary of Apollo at Triopio, Cnidos. Other participants in the alliance were Halicarnassos, Cnidos and three cities on Rhodes – Kamiros, Lindos and Ialysos. Kos was already famous in antiquity for its fertile soil. As an agricultural area it carried on limited commercial activities almost until the 4th century BC, in contrast to the neighbouring cities of Rhodes and the shores of Asia Minor. Its limited

Epicharmos (550-460 BC)

The first Greek comedy writer about whom we have clear information. He was born on Kos and lived in Syracuse, although according to some sources, the latter was also his birthplace. Around 500 BC, 35 years after Thespis, 11 years after the appearance of Phrynicus and immediately before the appearance of Aeschylus as a tragedian, Epicharmos produced the first comedy. Earlier, this area of drama had constituted nothing more than a collation of rude songs and sarcastic episodes, without plot and cohesion. Epicharmos gave a unity to the production and replaced the banal speeches with normal dialogue. His comedies, as is apparent from the 35 extant titles, were mostly parodies of mythological themes, although those with a political content were not absent. As opposed to tragedy, which gave emphasis to the pain suffered by the heroes and to the majesty of the gods, Epicharmos wanted to raise the spirits of the public by presenting humorous subject-matter clothed in the formality of the new theatrical art. Advancing beyond the hitherto low level of humour and the simple ribaldries of comedy, Epicharmos opened the way to parody of the usual themes of tragedy. Thus, the great changes which he brought defined him as the discoverer of comedy, although Phormis must have preceded him by a number of years. Whichever way it was, his excellence was so great that Plato described him as the 'king' of comedy writers. He died at the age of 90/97 years.

commerce was due both to the lack of a coastal city and to the absence of harbour installations until 366 BC, when the city of Kos was founded on the north-east shore of the island; there is no evidence for the existence of a Koan 'harbour post' on the shore of Asia Minor opposite the island, either in the Hellenistic or the Roman period. In general, accounts of the political history of Kos are limited in number; subjugation to, or alliance with, foreign powers constituted the main themes of the political history of the island in antiquity, and it is thus apparent that the island did not constitute a political or military power. During the later years of the archaic period and in the 5th century BC, the weakness of Kos is shown first by its subjugation to Persia and Halicarnassos and subsequently by its vassal alliance with Athens. Kos fell under the domination of the Persians immediately after their landing in Greece. Herodotus mentions that around 490 BC there was a tyrant-ruler on the island named Skythis, who was succeeded by his son Kadmos. Although the Persians supported this dynasty, Kadmos resigned and gave up the tyranny, wishing to give the island its independence. In 480 BC the tyrant of Halicarnassos, Artemisia, established her hegemony on Kos and the neighbouring islands of Kalymnos and Nisyros. Under this state of affairs, that is with alliances with the smaller islands and under the command of Artemisia, Kos fought on the side of the Persians at the sea battle of Salamis in 480 BC. Although we do not know exactly how long Kos remained under the domination of the Persians, it appeared in 451/450 as a member of the 'Delian League' and remained an ally of Athens until the end of the 5th century BC. A characteristic witness to the wealth and prosperity of Kos at the end of the archaic and beginning of the classical period is its silver coinage, which was already in circulation from the 6th century BC and bore the emblem of the island, the crab, with an impressed square on the obverse. On the silver coins of the 5th century BC, known by the name of 'discus-throwers', the crab has been relegated to the reverse while on the obverse there is the naked male figure of a discus-thrower which may be copied from a statue dating from the period. With the beginning of the Peloponnesian War in 412 BC, Kos found itself on the side of Athens. At that time, because the island lay defenseless after a terrible earthquake had struck, the Spartan general Astyochos was easily able to lay waste to it as he passed through on his way to Cnidos. The distancing of Rhodes from its alliance with Athens in 411 BC weakened the position of Kos against that strong city; thus the Athenian Alcibiades, on his way to Samos, razed Kos for a second time within the space of two years. Notwithstanding the fact that Alcibiades laid waste to Kos yet again in 407 BC, the alliance of Kos with Sparta does not seem to have been made before 394 BC. In general, Kos is characterized in the archaic period and the 5th century BC by a complete absence of political and economic development. This contrasts with the intellectual peak reached at the end of the 5th century which was marked by the establishment of the famous Medical School; the Koan doctor Hippocrates (460-370 BC) laid the foundations of medicine as a science based on methodical knowledge and the precepts of sound logic. Through his teachings, he inspired the foundation of the local medical school on Kos, which was to play a fundamental role in the development of medicine in antiquity. At the same time, great interest was shown in art, and found its expression through the creation of sculptures and reliefs of superb quality.

Hippocrates

The famous Greek physician and the father of Medicine, Hippocrates was born on Kos around 460 BC. On his father's side, he was the descendant of Asklepios in the 18th or 19th generation; on the side of his mother, Phainareti, he was descended from

Hippocrates, in an engraving from the Louvre.

Herakles in the 20th generation. As a member of the family of the Asklepiades he possessed that medical knowledge which was passed in great secrecy from father to son. As a physician he travelled to many parts of Greece, and indeed it was said that he was in Athens during the Peloponnesian War, where he was taught by the sophists Gorgias and Prodikos. He also took lessons from Democritos of Abdera and placed great importance on his philosophical education, since he believed that "a philosopher-doctor resembles God". Towards the end of his life he lived in Thessaly and on Thasos, and died around 377 BC in Larisa at the age of 104 or 109. According to the evidence of history and historical researchers, the tomb of this great physician of antiquity continued to exist outside

name of Hippocrates. His theoretical training was matched by his practical training and he never ceased to be interested in learning at all levels. With his work and his writings he condemned 'magic' medicine and laid the foundations for medicine as a science. He is closely connected with the Asklepeion on Kos and with a body of practical medical knowledge known as the Hippocratic Corpus. He was the founder of the School of 'the scientific art of therapy'; many of the texts which were used there were ascribed to him personally. 72 works written in Ionic and old Attic dialects bear his name and constituted a collection long before they came to the attention of the Alexandrine philologists, even though there is doubt about how many of them were actually written by him. It is considered likely that some of them were written by eminent doctors who surrounded Hippocrates, as well as by his sons Thessalos and Drakon, his grandchildren and his nephew Polybios. The most well-known of his works is the 'Aphorisms', a work which was highly valued in antiquity and the middle ages. It contains little suggestions

Larisa until the end of the 19th century. There is certainly one witness who recorded that in 1826, on the road from Larisa to Tyrnavo, there was a larnax (sarcophagus) and an inscription which clearly mentioned the

Engraving by J.B. Hilaire which depicts Hippocrates' Plane Tree Square. M.G.F.A. de Choiseul-Gouffier, Voyage pittoresque de la Grèce, Paris 1822.

relating to the nature of diseases, symptoms, crises and the final result. The treatise "On Airs, Waters, and Places" is of general interest and considered one of the most important of his works. It deals with the influence of the climate and water, and of the moulding of the natural environment on the physical and mental state of its inhabitants. In the second part of the same work the beginnings of comparative ethnography are discernible; the acuteness and accuracy of the observations are surprising.

Hippocrates attitude to cleanliness was revolutionary. When a plague broke out, he advised people to burn their clothes and to boil water before drinking it; it took more than 2,000 years for this vital practice finally to be rediscovered. He wrote on diagnostic methods, dietary traditions, the importance of hygiene, prevention of diseases, surgery, gynaecological conditions, and the topography and planning of cities; amongst many other things, he wrote that the human environment should be a healthy one.

The most important of his extant writings is the **Hippocratic Oath**:

THE HIPPOCRATIC OATH

"I SWEAR BY APOLLO THE PHYSICIAN AND BY ASKLEPIOS, HYGEIA AND PANACEA AND ALL THE OTHER GODS AND GODDESSES WHOM I CALL AS WITNESSES, THAT IN ACCORDANCE WITH MY POWER AND MY JUDGMENT I WILL FULFILL THIS OATH AND BOND:

- THAT I WILL CONSIDER THE ONE WHO TAUGHT ME THIS CRAFT TO BE EQUAL TO MY PARENTS, I WILL MAKE HIM A PARTICIPANT IN MY LIFE AND I WILL SHARE MY POSSESSIONS WITH HIM, IF NECESSARY. I WILL ALSO CONSIDER HIS SONS AS MY BROTHERS AND I WILL TEACH THEM THIS CRAFT, IF THEY WISH TO LEARN IT, WITHOUT PAYMENT OR CONDITIONS.

- THAT I WILL HAND ON THE CANONS OF THE PROFESSION TO MY SONS AND TO THE SONS OF MY TEACHER AND TO THE PUPILS WHO HAVE ENLISTED IN, AND PLEDGED THEMSELVES TO THE CANONS OF, THE PROFESSION, AND TO NOBODY ELSE.

- THAT I WILL USE THERAPEUTIC DIETS FOR THE BENEFIT ONLY OF THE SICK; IN ACCORDANCE WITH MY POWER AND JUDGMENT I WILL PROTECT THEM FROM EVERY HURT AND INJUSTICE.

I WILL NOT GIVE DEATH-BRINGING MEDICINE TO ANY PERSON, EVEN IF I AM ASKED FOR IT, NOR WILL I GIVE SUCH COUNSEL. SIMILARLY, I WILL NOT GIVE A MEDICINE TO A WOMAN TO PROVOKE ABORTION.

I WILL KEEP MY LIFE AND THE PRACTICE OF MY CRAFT PURE AND CLEAN. AND I WILL NOT OPERATE ON THOSE WHO SUFFER FROM STONES, BUT I WILL LEAVE THIS PRACTICE TO THOSE WHO HAVE ALREADY EXERCISED IT.

TO HOUSES TO WHICH I AM SUMMONED, I WILL GO FOR THE BENEFIT OF THE SICK, KEEPING MYSELF ABOVE ANY INTENTIONAL INJUSTICE OR OTHER CORRUPTION AND IN PARTICULAR DISTANT FROM ANY APHRODISIAC PRACTICE ON THE PERSONS OF WOMEN OR MEN, FREE OR SLAVES.

WHATEVER I SEE OR HEAR DURING THE PERIOD OF TREATMENT OR BEYOND, ABOUT THOSE THINGS WHICH SHOULD NOT BE MADE PUBLIC I WILL KEEP SILENT, IN THE BELIEF THAT THEY ARE SACRED SECRETS.

AS LONG, THEREFORE, AS I KEEP THIS OATH AND DO NOT BREAK IT, MAY I HAVE SUCCESS IN MY LIFE AND THE PRACTICE OF MY CRAFT, ALWAYS ENJOYING A GOOD REPUTATION AMONG MEN. IF AGAIN I BREAK IT AND EXCEED IT, MAY THE OPPOSITE BE THE CASE."

Silver coin of Kos with the crab on the reverse and the legend 'ΚΩΙΟΝ'. 357-330 BC.

The 4th century, until the death of Alexander the Great

During the 4th century BC, the most important event on Kos was the settlement and the foundation of the capital, the city of Kos (366/5 BC), which flourished and reached its peak of prosperity during the Hellenistic and Roman periods. As we have said, the alliance with Sparta took place at the beginning of the 4th century (around 394 BC), immediately after the defeat of the Athenians at the battle of Aigospotami. The situation must have remained stable until around 366/5, when the Second Athenian League was founded without the participation of the Koans; its goal was to oppose the imperialism of the Spartans. Kos participated in the war of 347/5 against Athens on the side of the disaffected allies, amongst which were Rhodes and Chios. Although its participation is not commented on by contemporary sources such as Isokrates and Demosthenes, this does not mean that it was an unimportant fighting power. It is probable that no mention was made of Kos because it fought on the side of former allies of Athens which had now rebelled. Undoubtedly, the most important event of the period was the internal strife which erupted on Kos in 366/5 and coincided in time with the foundation of the new capital of Kos on the north-eastern shore of the island. It is not clear whether this conflict was a consequence of the consolidation of settlement on the island or of the moving of the capital city in an already consolidated

city-state. Some assert that the description of *Diodoros (XV 76, 2)* and *Strabo (657)* about the moving of the capital city in itself reflects the movement from Astypalaia to Kos and not a real consolidation of settlement. Others speak of a consolidated state already in existence in the 5th century, since in the list of the Dorian Pentapolis as evidenced by *Herodotus (I, 144, 3)* mention is made of the participation of Kos as a unified island and not that of individual cities as in the case of Rhodes, where Kamiros, Lindos and Ialysos participated as independent cities. Another proof of the existence of a unified state from the 5th century BC onwards can undoubtedly be considered to exist from the coins, the so-called 'discus-throwers' with the legend *ΚΟΣ* or *ΚΩΣ* and later on *ΚΩΙΟΝ*. The inscriptions on the coinage indicate that it is not that of only one city, but of the whole island. There is, of course, the view that the unified coinage does not of necessity reflect a political unity, but rather an accepted economic agreement between several independent cities. Whatever was the case, it is certain that in 366 BC the capital was transferred to the north-east shore of the island, to an area in which the existence of settlement has been discerned already in the archaic period and the 5th century BC. Researchers, always mindful of the archaeological evidence, support the belief that this settlement must have been located immediately below the area of the Hellenistic and modern city and probably, until 366 BC, bore the name to which Thucydides referred, i.e. *Kos Meropis*. It is probable that before 366 BC, there was at least one other city – walled *Astypalaia* - besides the latter. We have no other information about the existence of more cities in the archaic period and 5th century BC. By contrast, there is evidence for the existence of the following 'demes' in the Hellenistic period, namely those of the Isthmiotes, Alasarnites, Phyxiotes, and Hippiotes, and the deme of the Antimachides, Aigilioi and Archides. The

The modern settlement complex of Asfendiou, centre of the ancient 'deme' of the Phyxiotes.

centre of the deme of the Isthmiotes was Astypalaia; the modern village of Asfendio was the centre of the deme of the Phyxiotes and Pyxiotes, and Antimahia was the centre of the triple deme of the Antimachides, Aigilioi and Archides. There are indications that some of the settlements in these demes already existed in the archaic period; one such example is Alasarna (modern Kardamaina) which constituted the religious centre of the island. Generally however, it is very difficult to complete the map of the cities of Kos before 366 BC and, as already mentioned, the only certain places are Kos Meropis, Astypalaia and Alasarna. Kos Meropis, which declined around 750 BC due to the movement of the population to fortified Astypalaia, experienced a revival at the end of the 6th century/ beginning of the 5th century BC due to the annexation of Kos to the dynasty of Lygdamis of Halicarnassos. This city was destroyed in 412 BC by the very strong earthquake which, according to Thucydides, shook the island at the time, and was almost rebuilt with the founding of Kos in 366 BC. The new, walled city concentrated together the larger part of the population which until then had been divided between Kos Meropis, Astypalaia, Alasarna, and some areas of the interior. A vast number of theories have been put forward about this settlement consolidation.

According to one of them, it came about as a riposte to Mausolus for the settlement which he established at Halicarnassos. Mausolus had succeeded his father in 377/6 BC and ruled Karia as a satrap until his death in 353/2. At the same time, he extended his kingdom to the Greek cities to the north, as well as to the south in eastern Lycia. Around 358/7 BC he incorporated Rhodes and Kos into his possession and developed relations with many other Greek areas, such as Chios and Knossos in Crete. Although there is no evidence, it is considered unlikely that the neighbouring islands to Kos – Nisyros, Kalymnos and Tilos – escaped occupation by him. The extension of his political power among the Greek islands is apparent from the fact that in 362 BC he transferred his capital form Mylasa, which was situated inland, to coastal Halicarnassos, which he strengthened through the application of an ambitious architectural programme and fortified with a strong wall. This 'refounding' and strengthening of Halicarnassos most probably created a

Modern Kardamaina (ancient Alasarna), as seen from the castle of Antimahia.

sense of panic on Kos and provoked the consolidation of the settlements there. However, according to Diodorus, the transfer of the capital city to Halicarnassus benefitted Kos economically, as shown by the trade in wine which increased during the second half of the 4th century BC. The influence of Mausolus on Kos is demonstrated by the coinage of the island. In particular, one series of tetradrachms which have been dated to around 357/353 BC depicts Herakles on the obverse with the facial features of Mausolus himself. The lack of similar coins on Chios and Rhodes bears witness to the priority given by Mausolus to the exercise of rule over the nearest island - Kos – and to the further extension of his influence thereafter. Even though the evidence is scanty, it is certain that the settlement consolidation on Kos served its purpose, which was the economic strengthening of the island. The existence of wealthy families is demonstrated by the group of statues at Olympia which depict the Koan Olympic victors Xenovrotos and Xenodikos, as well as by the evidence of a large number of economic

Silver tetradrachm with Herakles on the obverse and the crab on the reverse. 356-300 BC.

loans made by some Koans to the inhabitants of Kalymnos.
Kos, together with Chios and Rhodes, fought under the command of Mausolus against Athens (357-355 BC), with the goal of restricting Athenian imperialism. After the war, Mausolus extended his domination over Rhodes and Kos by establishing a military presence which naturally wounded the existing democratic order. For its part, Athens concentrated on the struggle against Philip of Macedon and was not concerned with what was happening in the south-eastern Aegean. In 333 BC, Kos found itself in the hands of the Persian satrap Orontovates, heir to the throne of Karia. Following his victory at Granikos in 334 BC, Alexander the Great began to advance southwards, conquering the Greek cities of Asia Minor. After a fierce struggle, he managed to gain the upper hand in the city of Halicarnassos while the Persians

who had been driven out retreated to Kos and strengthened the defenses of the island. In 332 BC however, the Macedonians definitively ejected the Persians from the Aegean and 'took' Kos, after an invitation by the Koans themselves who wanted to demonstrate their pro-Macedonian sympathies. The situation on Kos under the domination of Alexander is generally obscure; we do not know whether the Macedonians installed some kind of military fort after the occupation, as happened on Rhodes. Even more obscure is the relationship of Alexander himself with Kos, although we know that two Koans participated on his expedition to India: Kritovoulos, most probably the physician who had previously saved the sight of Philip, and Kritodemos who was Alexander's personal physician. It should be mentioned here that in 337 BC, a number of Koans left the island and settled in Greek cities in Sicily, such as Gela, which was a colony of people from Rhodes and Crete. The possibility cannot be excluded that this movement reflected economic and social problems on the island.

23

Apelles (c. 352-308 BC)

The most famous Greek painter of antiquity. According to a number of authors he was born on Kos, while others believe that he originated from Ephesos or Colophona in Ionia. According to historical accounts, he produced unique works of art, although none of them have survived. He was a contemporary of Alexander and the only one whom the latter permitted to paint his portrait.

Alexander the Great and Cambases in the workshop of the painter Apelles. A painting by Giovanni Batista Tiepolo, 1740.

Amongst many of such portraits produced by him was one depicting **Alexander** with a thunderbolt in his hand, which hung in the temple of Artemis at Ephesos. A tradition describes that Alexander objected when he saw one of the portraits of himself, considering that it was not a good likeness. However, when his horse whinnied at the sight of the portrait, Apelles declared that the horse understood more about art than its master. Apelles was widely concerned with mythological subject-matter, although he is considered to have been the first artist in the world to paint his self-portrait. Although we do not know exactly when and where Apelles died, we are in a position to acknowledge that he spent his life studying and improving the technique of painting. In his most famous work – 'Aphrodite rising from the waves' - the drops of water falling from the wet hair of the goddess formed a silvery, translucent covering around her. They say that the model for the work was **Cambases**, one of the mistresses of Alexander the Great. Apelles used to say to his colleagues that they had all the necessary prerequisities to become artists except for one – 'grace' – which he believed that only he possessed.

The period following the death of Alexander the Great (the years from 323 BC to 286 BC)

After the death of Alexander the Great in 323 BC, wars broke out between his successors and the Greek cities took sides, supporting one or the other heir. Originally Kos supported Ptolemy of Egypt, then later Antigonos Monophthalmos (Antigonos the one-eyed). According to references by Diodorus, when war broke out in 315 BC between Antigonos and the alliance of Seleukos, Ptolemy, Kassandros and Lysimachos, Seleukos and Ptolemy hastened to help Kassandros to conquer Limnos which had broken away from Antigonos. The attempt was unsuccessful and on the return journey Seleukos anchored in the open harbour of Kos which welcomed him and his ally, Ptolemy. In 309 BC Ptolemy 'took' Kos, probably without any opposition, in that the island, following the model of Rhodes, took a friendly stance. Like Rhodes - so Kos; thanks to that friendly stance the Koans participated in the development of important trade relations with Alexandria. Ptolemy II, named Philadelphos, son of Ptolemy and

Berenice, was born on Kos. He was taught by the great thinker of the period, the famous Philetes, who also accompanied his pupil to Alexandria itself and continued his teachings there. In the spring of 308 BC Ptolemy Soter left for Egypt and shortly afterwards contacts began between Kos and Antigonos. After the battle of Ipsos (301 BC) and the territorial redistributions embarked upon by the successors of Alexander, Kos seems to have remained under the influence of Antigonos. During the period of the Macedonian occupation, Kos actually remained independent, retaining its own laws.

Erondas or Erodas

A composer of iambic verse who lived on Kos in the 3rd century BC. Little was known of his work until the recent discovery of seven poems in papyri in the British Museum. The titles of the seven poems are: Proxenites and Mastropos (literally meaning 'procurer and pimp'), Pornovoskos (literally meaning 'whoremonger-shepherd'), Teacher, Visit to the Asklepeion, Zilotypos (literally meaning 'a jealous man'), Friends and Trusted Ones, and the Cobbler. The poems are difficult to read, full of words of which some are completely unknown, while others are only met in Hesychios. The possibility that some of these words are the results of mistakes by the Egyptian copyists who produced the papyri cannot be excluded.

Ptolemy Philadelphos (309-246 BC).

Kos and the Ptolemies
(286 – 197 BC)

After the defeat of Demetrios in 286 BC, Ptolemy achieved supremacy over the whole of the Aegean Sea, while the occupation of Tyre and Sidon ensured him control of Phoenicia. This period also saw a warming of relations between the Ptolemaic dynasty and Kos. Certainly from 280 BC until the end of the following decade, Ptolemy Philadelphos had regained all the influence which his father, Ptolemy Soter, had had on the whole Aegean area. In relation to the new political situation, it should be noted that Kos was not subject to the Ptolemies in the sense that the other territories in Asia Minor and the Greek islands were, since no regime of supervisory government, defense or taxation was in force. The autonomy of Kos during this period is recalled with emphasis in the work of Erondas, who was writing iambic verse at the time. The economic flowering of the island which is demonstrated by the rebuilding of the city and development in the various 'demes' is due to the exemption in part from taxes by the Ptolemies. There is no clear evidence pertaining to the official relations of the Koans with Ptolemy Philadelphos and the later Ptolemies; nevertheless, apart from the apparent good relations with Philadelphos and his successors Philopater and Epiphanes, the Ptolemies are mentioned as allies of the island at the end of the 3rd century BC. It is not impossible that the origin of the goodwill that the Ptolemies showed towards Kos was due to a respect which they felt towards the birthplace, not only of medicine, but also of

Philadelphos himself. This close relationship is evidenced not only in philological sources, such as the writings of the poet Callimachus, but also in inscriptions, for example that which mentions the dispatch of corn to Kos at a time of need by King Ptolemy (either Philadelphos or Euergetes). There is also evidence that during the reign of Philadelphos the personal physician of the king, a Koan, was honoured for his services. For their part, the Koans expressed their confidence in Philadelphos in the posthumous worship they reserved for his sister, Queen Arsinoe. She died in 267 BC and was worshipped throughout Egypt and beyond, in the areas which were under the influence of the Ptolemies. The friendly relations between the two areas are witnessed by the exchanges which took place on the intellectual level in the

form of Koan teachers and physicians of the royal family, as well as by the foundation of a royal school of medicine in Alexandria whose staff comprised great scientific capacities from Kos. It should be mentioned that the Koan residents of Alexandria not only remembered their place of origin, but constituted a binding link between the Ptolemaic dynasty and the island. Apart from the intellectuals, doctors, teachers and writers, people of lower status such as soldiers who had served in the army of the Ptolemies also went to Alexandria from Kos. For a short interlude, after the war of 265/260 in which Antigonos Gonatas defeated Ptolemy Philadelphos, the Koans most probably distanced themselves from the kingdom of Egypt; however, after

The Temple of Asklepios (3rd century BC). The Asklepeion was finished immediately after the restoration of relations between the island and Ptolemy Euergetes in 242 BC.

242 BC the relations of the island with Ptolemy Euergetes were restored. In the same period, the Asklepeion was completed and the Koans founded the Panhellenic festival of Asklepios. By sending out Theoroi to all the kings and the city states to demand that the sanctuary be designated a 'place of immunity', they achieved international recognition for the Sanctuary and Festival. A few years later, when Ptolemy Euergetes ruled Egypt (246-222/1 BC), the interest of the Macedonian king Antigonos of Doson (229-221 BC) was kindled in Karia. During this period, and after a number of his successes, there is evidence that he was both present and also worshipped on Kos, although we know nothing about the good deeds which provoked that worship. Whatever was the case, the presence of the Macedonian king on the island does not seem in the least to have influenced its relations with the Ptolemies at the end of the 3rd century BC. At this time, Rhodes appeared on the stage as a new trading and naval power. Kos appears to have followed her, again without creating problems in its relationships with the Ptolemies. Kos took part on the side of Rhodes in the First Cretan War, which broke out in 205 BC between Rhodes and the Cretan cities because they had been harrassing Rhodian trading ships through pirate activity. It also sided with Rhodes in the subsequent war (201/200 BC) against Philip V of Macedon who, after northern Greece, the Hellespont and Propontis, turned his gaze upon the central Aegean and western Asia Minor. The evident abandonment of the acropolis of Alasarna (modern Kardamaina) and of Nisyros exactly opposite was due to the attacks by Philip. Others followed on Rhodes and Karia until the spring of 200 BC, when Philip V was forced to leave the region and return to Macedon which now found itself under threat of Roman occupation. It should be mentioned here that in the meanwhile, already at the time of the First Cretan War (205 BC), Kos had incorporated the hitherto independent island of Kalymnos, forming what is referred to in the literary sources as the 'Omopolitia' which continued to exist during the Roman period. After the end of the Second Macedonian War in 197 BC, the Ptolemies lost a significant number of their territories in the Aegean. This, together with a series of internal conflicts which brought about the weakness of the dynasty, led to the end of their domination on Kos. Thereafter Rhodes took over their position, themselves to be superseded later on by the Romans.

Silver dekadrachm with Arsinoe II, sister and wife of Ptolemy Philadelphos, on the obverse and a double 'horn of plenty' on the reverse. 260 BC.

Ptolemy Philadelphos,
king of Egypt

Son of Ptolemy I and Berenice, born on Kos in 309 BC. He became embroiled in war with Magas, his half-brother and the son of Berenice from her first marriage, who ruled in Cyrene after pressure had been exerted by Berenice on her husband, Ptolemy I. After the death of his mother Magas, aspiring to the power of the Ptolemies, rose in revolt against his brother Ptolemy Philadelphos and came to an understanding with Antiochos of Syria who was already at war with Philadelphos. His attempts not only failed to come to fruition, but three years later Magas was forced to make peace with Ptolemy Philadelphos, promising that Cyrenaica would no

Ptolemy Philadelphos frees Jewish prisoners as a remuneration for the translation of the Old Testament into Greek. Medieval hand engraving, 15th century.

longer be the object of his intentions; to set a seal to the treaty, he would give his own daughter, Berenice, in marriage to Ptolemy, son of Philadelphos. However, after the death of Magas his wife Apami, daughter of Antiochos I of Syria, refused to give her daughter to Ptolemy and instead chose as a bridegroom for her Demetrios Kalos (Demetrios the Good) who was the brother of Antigonos Gonatas, king of Macedon. Thus Cyrenaica passed under the influence of the Macedonian sphere, excluding Ptolemy Philadelphos from power over it; in any case, the latter at that particular time wanted to avoid any kind of clash with Gonatas. A few years later Ptolemy Euergetes, son of Philadelphos, supported a conspiracy by Berenice against her husband Demetrios who had had a relationship with her mother, Apami, and they killed him. Thus it was that with great ease, Ptolemy Euergetes became lord of Cyrene, and after his marriage to Berenice, he united it with Egypt.

Ptolemy Philadelphos made a treaty with the Romans; hostilities with Syria ceased towards the end of his reign and he married his daughter Berenice to Antiochus II. In addition to the government of his kingdom, Philadelphos was greatly interested in literature and science. The 'Museum of Alexandria' to which intellectuals from all over the world came, contained the famous library with all the treasures of ancient literature. He had a great love for nature and also took the decision to translate the Old Testament from Hebrew into Greek. He founded a large number of colonies and cities along the boundaries of his kingdom; on the Red Sea alone he founded at least two named Arsinoe, one named after his other sister Philotera, and two after his mother, Berenice. He founded cities of the same name in Cilicia and Syria, and in Palestine, the mighty city of Ptolemais. Generally, there is no doubt that during his lifetime, Egypt achieved brilliance and power which could be measured in many soldiers, horses, ships and talents.

After he banished his first wife Arsinoe who was accused of conspiracy, he married his own sister, also called Arsinoe. With his first wife he had two sons - Ptolemy his heir, and Lysimachos - and one daughter, Berenice, who married Antiochus of Syria.

The Economy of the Hellenistic Period

When we cast a glance at the daily life of the people and the economy of Kos during antiquity, we quickly discern that most of the information we have available refers to the 3rd and 2nd centuries BC, i.e. the Hellenistic period; the reason is that Kos achieved its greatest flowering and prosperity during those centuries. This is shown indisputably by the vigorous building activity of the period which included the Asklepeion, numerous temples and altars, the extension of the market-place and its embellishment with shops and stoas, the fortification of Alasarna, and many other public works. The private residences of well-to-do citizens of the period are also impressive, with marble furniture and mosaics of high artistic quality. It was mainly this development which led to the foundation of the new capital in 366 BC on the north-eastern shore of the island, exactly on the great trading route from the Black Sea to the East. The new city was built just at the right time and together with its enclosed harbour, launched the trading activities and increased the income of the island. On the other hand, political stability and the export of wine and amphorae were two other definitive factors of development. The lack of data prevents us from knowing how long the prosperity of the 3rd and 2nd century lasted. Nevertheless, even if the proclamation by the Romans of the harbour of Delos as a free port led to a reduction of traffic in the harbour at Kos and surely dealt its economy a significant blow, we cannot say that Kos suffered economically after its occupation by the Romans. In fact, it retained its freedom and was exempted from taxation up to the time of Augustus.

A basic source of wealth for Kos, even in antiquity, was its agricultural production, since the fertility of its soils was famous and proverbial. To the income from the latter there should be added some wealth from the mining of metals, even though the information about these is limited. In addition to vine-growing and olive oil production an important sector of agricultural activity was the cultivation of grain. As the farming region par excellence, it was logical that the wealth of the inhabitants should be defined on the basis of the amount of property they owned. Inscriptions give us a good picture of the occupations of the island inhabitants: shop owners, retail merchants, tax collectors, courtesans, artists, craftsmen, physicians, and of course, farmers and fishermen.

The system of taxation operated on the island is of particular interest. According to one inscription, there were two kinds of taxes: direct taxes and income from public property. Foodstuffs such as grain, bread and dried fish were taxable. A certain type of wine from Kos was also taxed, as well as wine from Kalymnos. The same was true for wood, wool and animals (quadrupeds). The owners of vineyards also paid taxes for the slaves who worked for them, as did the owners of brothels and courtesans, incense vendors, sellers of jewellery, murex, and fish, as well as many others. This well-developed system of taxation has erroneously been associated with the presence of the Ptolemies on the island; Kos clearly maintained its autonomy during this period in many ways, and the system employed was vastly different to that of any Egyptian prototype.

Another sector of the economy of Kos is of great interest – the guilds. Inscriptions refer to guilds of physicians (Asklepiades) which already existed from the archaic period onwards, as well as guilds of potters and bronze-smiths. There were two basic spheres of pottery production: that of female figurines and that of amphorae. In particular the latter, apart from covering the shipping requirements where the famous Koan wine was concerned, were also exported and subject to great demand.

The Roman domination of Kos (192-32 BC)

Tetradrachm with the portrait of Eumenes II of Pergamon.

With the establishment of Roman supremacy in Greece and Asia Minor from 200 BC onwards Kos, following the example of Rhodes, expressed its belief in the new power, thus somehow managing to preserve its 'autonomy' as a city-state as it had been in the past.

It is not certain whether the Koan fleet helped the Romans in the Second Macedonian War, even though there are clear indications

The Romans defeated the fierce king of Macedon, Philip V, at Kynos Kefales in 197 BC. Kos fought on the side of Rome in this battle.

that Kos fought on their side. It held the same position in the war between Rome and Antiochus III (192-190 BC), who began to expand his territory to the detriment of important allies of Rome, such as Eumenes II of Pergamon. After the Treaty of Apameia in 188 BC the prosperous state of Pergamon controlled

Kos, which reacted positively by declaring a public festival in honour of king Eumenes II. Rhodes was experiencing economic problems mainly because the Romans had downgraded their harbour and thus strengthened the position of Delos, proclaiming it 'autonomous' in 171 BC. By contrast Kos, which would in no way ever have constituted a strategic threat to the Romans, remained almost untouched by the results of the war. One of the changes which Roman domination brought to the island seems to have concerned the coinage of the second half of the 2nd century BC, which was now silver and in line with the Athenian and Rhodian system. At the same time, the friendly relations between Kos and the Ptolemies were not interrupted, as is shown by an inscription which describes rites celebrated on

the premises of the Gymnasion in their honour. In addition, Koan citizens continued to be found in Alexandria, living there as high officials of the royal court.

Apart from those it maintained with the Ptolemies, Kos had friendly relations with other Hellenistic kingdoms, such as that of Bithynia, both at the time of Nicodemos II (149-127 BC) and earlier, during the reign of Nicodemos I (280-250 BC), mainly for reasons of trade in the Black Sea. It is believed that a friendly relationship also probably existed with the Seleucid kingdom during the reign of Antiochos VIII, who was said to have discovered the antidote for snake-bite; the latter is mentioned in an inscription which has been found at the Asklepeion on Kos. The meteoric development of the Asklepeion during the 2nd century BC, according to some studies, was due to the donations given to it by

Hellenistic rulers who had contacts with Kos regarding the erection of buildings. The next big war in which the Koans were involved was the First Pontic War with Mithridates. This king, also named Eupator, was born in 132 BC in Amaseia, capital of the satrapy of Pontos. He was the son of the Persian Mithridates V and Laodikeia, a daughter of the Seleucids. In 88 BC he began the First Pontic War against the Roman Empire, hoping that he would be able to proceed as far as the conquest of Rome itself. Within a short space of time, his general Archelaos

Mithridates Eupator. Sketch from a coin of the period.

had conquered all of Asia Minor, the islands of the Aegean, eastern Greece and all of Macedonia which this time fought on the side of the Romans. In 87 BC the Roman general Sulla arrived in Greece with 30,000 men and after a siege lasting one year, captured Athens and Piraeus. Thereafter, in 85 BC the

Pontic army of general Archelaos was defeated by Sulla in decisive battles at Chaironeia and Orchomenos.
In 88 BC Mithridates, king of Pontos, after he had conquered almost all of Asia Minor, slaughtered more than 80,000 Romans; he sailed against Kos and Rhodes with the intention of dispersing their fleets and taking his revenge on the areas which had harboured Roman fugitives. He did not manage to attack Rhodes, thanks to the good fortification of the island. On Kos, however, he gave vent to his anger, taking prisoner Ptolemy VIII, the grandson of Cleopatra, wife of Ptolemy Euergetes, and seizing the treasure which she had given to the Asklepeion for safe-keeping. Even though some support the view that he did not cause serious damage to the city and that the citizens rendered him honour, the only thing certain is that after his withdrawal, the Koans continued to maintain the best relations with the Romans and fought on their side in 86/5, to achieve the freedom of Chios and Samos from Mithridates. After the Civil War which erupted when Pompey came into conflict with Caesar (dissolving the triumvirate of Caesar,

From its relations with the conquerors it is apparent that Kos maintained the regime of an **autonomous** and **independent state**, in contrast to Rhodes. According to the historian Plutarch it is typical that the Roman general Lucullus demanded ships from the Rhodians, while from Kos - which had some type of autonomy - he asked for their support through the loan of part of their fleet. The same happened in the case of the general Sulla in 82 BC, who did not punish the island at all for the reception of honour it had given to Mithridates, one of the greatest enemies of the Roman state.

Pompey and Crassus) and the victory of Caesar in the decisive battle at Pharsala in 48 BC, we find the Koans paying honour not only to the victorious Caesar, but also to his friend, Gaius Julius Theopompus, by dedicating a statue to him in the Asklepeion. Caesar, however, was murdered and after many consultations the second triumvirate was established in 43 BC, consisting of Octavian, Anthony and Lepidus. After the latter was driven out, the other two divided the Roman empire between them;

Anthony received the East, and Octavian the West. They lost no time however, in fighting amongst themselves and thus, after the famous battle of Actium in 31 BC, Octavian (Augustus) became the sole ruler of the whole empire, which of course included Kos. During the years following the death of Caesar, the Koan Nikias had acquired great power on the island, although there were some who called him a tyrant. He was said to be very educated, and owned great property and herds; he had gone to Rome in 62 BC and lived among circles of intellectuals such as Cicero, Cassius and Brutus. When he returned to Kos he wore a diadem which had as its prototype that worn by the Hellenistic rulers, and he issued a coinage on which he was depicted wearing a crown. The period of his tyranny, which cannot have lasted more than eight years, fell within the period of the second triumvirate.

During the reign of the Emperor Augustus, the regime of the 'free city' which had hitherto prevailed on Kos finally came to an end. It was now a component of the Roman Empire and part of the Province of Asia. Extant information that the amount of the annual taxation now reached 1,000 talents indicates the economic flowering of the island, which thanks to the beneficence of Augustus was almost rebuilt at the end of the 1st century BC after terrible earthquakes had struck it. There is evidence that, for this reason, Augustus was worshipped in Kos as Apollo the Saviour and Protector of Property (*Apollon Sotiras and Ktisias*). In 23 AD the Senate recognized the 'immunity' of the Asklepeion, and in 53 AD the island was favoured by Claudius with a decision to exempt it from taxes. It is said that this decision had to do with his personal physician, the Koan Gaius Stertinius Xenophon, whom he considered to be a descendant of Asklepios.

Although the extant information regarding Kos is sporadic after the reign of Claudius, it is thought that the island regained its freedom after 79 AD. Mention of Kos as a 'free city' is found again during the reign of Caracalla; this state of affairs must have continued until the end of the period, with Kos enjoying complete prosperity thanks to the Pax Romana, the lucrative trade in silk, and the cultivation of its fruitful soils.

Bronze coin with the portrait of Nikias, the tyrant of Kos. c.30 BC.

In addition to great wealth, the **Koan Gaius Stertinius Xenophon** also acquired judicial and military rank and was honoured for his efforts; this was also extended to his whole family, both those members in Rome and back home on Kos. He reciprocated by financing private and public works on the island, such as the provision of the water supply to the Asklepeion, the library and a small temple in its central court. Thus he was named 'son of the deme', 'patriot', 'the pious', and 'benefactor', and a portrait of him was used as an emblem on the coinage of Kos. In Rome he was referred to as 'friend of Caesar', 'friend of Claudius' and 'friend of Rome', which clearly attests to the huge radiance of his personality.

Early Christian - Byzantine period

During the early Christian years many Koans embraced the new religion, and as was to be expected the Romans persecuted them vigorously and meted out harsh punishments. The period of the emperor Diocletian (284-305 AD) was one of particular barbarity; he was one of the greatest enemies of Christianity and many civil uprisings took place during his reign. However, Constantine the Great came onto the scene in 305 AD, having hitherto been governor of the western part of the Roman Empire along with Maxentius. Constantine defeated Maxentius and appears from then on to have demonstrated his sympathy for the new religion in his endeavours to exempt the Christians from the persecutions and torments. Following his actions and initiatives, the famous Edict of Milan (313 AD) was issued, which recognized religious tolerance and the free practice of the Christian religion. Thanks to the Edict, Christianity began to flower on Kos; it is said that the Apostle Paul came to the island in 57 AD and taught there beneath the plane tree in the Asklepeion. After the transfer of the capital of the eastern Roman Empire to Constantinople in 330 AD by Constantine, Kos became part of the Byzantine empire and belonged for administrative purposes to the area of the Dodecanese, as did Rhodes. The flowering and spread of Christianity on the island is witnessed by the number of early Christian basilicas there. At least 26 churches of this characteristic type have been located, scattered over the whole island; they attest both to the development of Christian communities there and to the economic prosperity of the epoch. Unfortunately, the great earthquake of 469 AD destroyed most of these monuments, which were constructed with ancient building material and decorated with

Capital from the early Christian basilica of Ayios Stefanos.

mosaics of impressive workmanship. They were rebuilt; however

Mosaic from the early Christian basilica in the western sector of excavations.

the island, and along with it the Asklepeion, was razed once again by a series of barbarian attacks by the Vandals (457-67), the Isauri (469/70), the Bulgars (527) and perhaps by the Persians of Hosroi II and the Arabs, as well as the catastrophic earthquake of 554 AD. A new period of decline began. Unfortunately, there is very little information extant about the island from the 7th to 11th centuries. According to one source, after the defeat of the Byzantines at Matzikert (1071) refugees trying to escape the fury of the Seljuk Turks began to flood the island. Amongst them was Hosios Christodoulos (the blessed Christodoulos) who established himself at Palaio Pyli. With contributions from the emperors Nikiforos Botaneiatis (1078-81) and Alexios Komninos (1081-1118) he managed to build a monastery. Later, in 1088, again with the agreement of Alexios Komninos, he presented it to Kos and received the island of Patmos in return. Another typical event in the 11th century was the revolt of Nikiforos Melissinous in 1081 which began from Kos, extended to the coast of Asia Minor opposite and was halted by Alexios Komninos himself outside Constantinople.

Frankish Domination and the Rule of the Knights

In the 12th century the Venetians spread their rule throughout the whole area of the Byzantine Empire and in 1204 managed to capture its capital, Constantinople. Thereafter they spread through the rest of Greece and the islands; Kos now constituted a Dukedom

The coat of arms at the entrance to the castle of Antimahia.

of the Venetian Republic which was administered by **Leon Gavalas**. The Frankish domination of the island was interrupted in 1261 when Michael Palaeologos ejected the Venetians and took back Constantinople. In the new Byzantine Empire, Kos was not part of any 'theme' (administrative area) but a separate part of the empire with its own governor who reported directly to the emperor. However, from the mid-13th century pirate attacks and pillaging began and it is mentioned that Kos itself was a base for the pirate fleet. In 1284, despite its fierce resistance, the island passed once more into the hands of the Venetians and became a Venetian territory

A coat of arms set into the wall of the fortress of the city of Kos.

governed by a castellan until the beginning of the 14th century, even though there is one view that the invasion was itself of a purely piratical nature, without any accompanying changes in government. In 1312 Kos was pillaged once more, by the Catalans, and in 1315 it passed into the hands of the Knights of the Order of St. John under the leadership of **Foulgie de Villaret**,

who gave the island the name of **Lango** and **Neratzia**, since many lemon and orange trees had been planted there. Like neighbouring Rhodes, Kos remained in the hands of the Knights for 208 years until 1523, when it was conquered by the Turks under Sultan Suleyman. Virtually nothing is known about the method of government of the island under the Knights, even though it is certain that there was a law court there. As is apparent from some archives, relations of the Order with the Monastery of Patmos were good; the monastery had possessions on Leros, but not on Kos. As on the other islands which were held by the Knights, a Latin bishop was established on Kos, while the Ecumenical Patriarch continued to send Orthodox prelates to the island. Another noteworthy event in this period, under the **Master D'Aubusson** (1476-1503), was the expulsion of all the Jews who had lived on the island for centuries, on grounds that they were a danger. During their rule, the Knights reinforced the defense of the island, building strong castles, with a view to dealing with attacks by the Turks and Egyptians. It is mentioned that the **Master Helion de Villeneuve** (1319-1346) built the castles of Neratzia and Antimahia. The governor on Kos in 1433 was **Fantino Querini di Stampalia**, who strengthened the island defenses and repulsed an attack by the Egyptian fleet in 1440. However, his move to demolish the houses near the castle of Neratzia provoked disturbances and general discontent which led to his removal from office in 1453. In the same year,

Part of the wall of the castle of Neratzia, with coats of arms set into it.

immediately after the sack of Constantinople by the Turks, the Ottoman fleet began its incursions and pillaging of the islands of the Aegean. On one of these expeditions, in 1457, the Turks captured the castle of Neratzia but were not able to advance to the castles at Antimahia, Palaio Pyli and Kefalos. Thus, after 23 days of fruitless siege, they laid waste to the island and left. A series of incursions followed until 1485, obliging many of the inhabitants of the island to move to Rhodes despite the objections of the government. Unfortunately, the reinforcement structures added to the defensive walls by the Knights in 1492 were razed together with nearly all the buildings on the island in the following year, when a terrible earthquake hit the island. The Turkish attacks did not cease, and on 6th January 1523 Kos passed into Turkish hands as a result of a treaty between Sultan Suleyman and the Knights of St. John, and the immediate withdrawal of the latter from Rhodes.

The fountain with the Arabic inscription in Plane Tree Square.

Turkish Domination

The withdrawal of the Knights of St. John in 1523 marked the beginning of a long period of Turkish occupation (390 years) on the island, with the introduction of its new name **'Stanköy'**,

The mosque of the Loggia in Plane Tree Square.

meaning 'on/to Kos'. Barbarism, expulsions, bloodshed and mass kidnapping of children – all of these characterized a whole period during which Hellenism and every intellectual activity on the island languished. As if that were not enough, when the Knights of St. John tried without success to recapture the island in 1603, the Turks pillaged it and sold the female prisoners they took in the slave markets of Tunisia. Despite the difficulties the island faced, including a terrible epidemic of the plague in 1811-14, the flame of Hellenism and

Christianity remained unquenched there, and fired the enthusiasm for participation by the island in the great struggle of the nation. When the Greek Revolt broke out in 1821, the contribution of the Koans cost the lives of 90 rebels who were hanged by the Turks in Platanos Square. Although the violence against the inhabitants continued, the intervention of Gerasimos, Archbishop of Kos pacified spirits at least until the end of the century, securing the conditions for commercial exchange with Crete, Alexandria and Constantinople.

Italian Occupation

Despite the struggles and its participation in the Greek Revolt of 1821 Kos, together with the other islands of the Dodecanese, continued

The building which today houses the National Tourist Organisation of Greece.

to be under Ottoman rule until 1912, when it fell into Italian hands. The Italians arrived on the island as liberators from the Turks and for this reason they were received enthusiastically by the Koans who hoped that the time for their union with the rest of Greece was nigh. Italy promised that its rule on the island would be of an interim nature and that during the period there would be complete respect for the religion and education of the inhabitants. Unfortunately however, the situation developed in a quite different way, particularly after the signing of the Treaty of Lausanne in 1923 in which Article 15 stated categorically that Turkey should cede

to Italy a number of islands, including Kos. As soon as Fascism prevailed, the original good intent of the occupiers turned into a real nightmare, since their goal now was the complete 'italicising' of public life. The local people lost their property and lived under conditions of economic degradation, while at the same time they were dealt a huge blow in matters of religion and education. The Italian language, which was only taught piecemeal in the schools, very slowly began to replace Greek completely, and in secondary schools only Italian was used. Thus Greek children in most cases remained uneducated, or they were forced to take lessons in Greek at schools held during the night, which were

The Government Building of Kos.

somewhat like the 'secret schools' that had existed under the Turkish occupation. The same barbarity was exercised in the field of religion, where the ordination of new Orthodox priests was completely forbidden, with the ulterior motive of quashing religious feeling. On top of these adverse conditions came the terrible earthquake of 1933 which razed the city to the ground. During the application of a programme of rebuilding which was based on Italian urban planning, the ancient city was discovered; the research, study and conservation of the archaeological treasures was entrusted - as was to be expected - to Italian archaeologists. The rebuilding was finished in 1936, leaving the wonderful public and private buildings

View of/from the central courtyard of the Government Building.

which embellish the city to this day. This difficult period in the history of Kos ended with the defeat of Italy in the Second World War; after the fall of Mussolini, British forces began to appear on the island.

Union with Greece

On 3rd October 1943, a few days after the arrival of British forces on Kos, the German fleet and air force attacked Kos and took it without difficulty, since the strength of

the British was small and resistance thus impossible. The German occupation was one of the toughest and most violent for the local population; because of the truly degrading conditions which prevailed people were obliged to move in droves to Asia Minor. The defeat of Germany in 1945 led to the obligatory surrender of the island to Britain. Kos, together with the other islands of the Dodecanese celebrated its long sought-after freedom, which culminated in the final union with Greece on 7th March, 1948.

The building which houses the Archaeological Museum.

THE CITY OF KOS

Detail of the clock of the 'Leschi' in Eleftheria Square.

Getting to know the city

The city of Kos has been inhabited without a break from about the middle of the 3rd millennium until the present day. As recent research has shown, occupation during the Bronze Age was centred on the Seraglio Hill in the middle of the modern city. It continued there during the Geometric and Archaic periods, despite the transfer of the capital to so-called *Kos Astipalaia*, on the southern shore of the island. Around 366 BC, when the consolidation took place on the island with the fusion of the older settlements, the capital 'returned' to the north-east shore and ancient *Kos Meropis* (i.e. modern Kos), which became (and still is) the administrative centre of the island. The city was walled and constructed in accordance with the Hippodamian system of town planning, that is with horizontally and vertically running streets which divided it into a grid of complete squares for building. The harbour was furnished with a separate wall. Unfortunately, the picture of the city has never remained static, due to the many earthquakes which have shaken it from antiquity to the present day. Nevertheless the building phases are detectable because of the materials used, which varied from period to period. For example, in the 3rd century BC limestone was the main building material, while marble predominated in the following century. The latter was the time of monumental buildings which were almost completely razed by the earthquake of 65 BC. Rebuilding followed, but the structures were in turn razed by an earthquake in 142 AD. In the next phase, Kos was enhanced with important buildings such as the baths, the Stadium and the theatre, while the market-place (Agora) was rebuilt at

The steps which lead from the Avenue of the Palms to Plane Tree Square.

network of streets and buildings of the ancient city was brought to light and important restoration work began, including that of the Odeion and the Roman house (Casa Romana). In addition, the main archaeological areas of the city were defined: the area of the market and the harbour, the altar of Dionysos and all of the western archaeological area. In order to facilitate their researches, the Italian archaeologists divided the area into archaeological zones, namely the eastern zone (harbour and agora), the western,

the same time. Finally, the earthquake of 469 AD dealt an irreparable blow to the ancient city, which almost vanished beneath the new buildings of the early Christian era; the final death-blow to the ancient city was administered by the earthquake of 554 AD. While this series of earthquakes caused all traces of the ancient city to be lost, it was a much later earthquake,

in 1933, which led to the unravelling of a vital lead to its rediscovery. Beneath the rubble, the Italian Archaeological School began excavations under the direction of the archaeologist *L. Laurenzi*, and subsequently *L. Morricone*. Thus, during the Italian occupation of the island, the

The harbour pulses with life every day.

Notable infrastructure projects were undertaken, such as the construction of wide roadways, the planting of trees, the erection of imposing public buildings such as the Government Building to the east of the castle, the public market and the 'leschi' in Eleftheria Square. The Avenue of the Palms and the stone

and the central zone; we will visit these zones below, in detail. Apart from the discovery of the ancient city, the catastrophic earthquake of 1933 provided a motive for yet another reconstruction, which this time was carried out to anti-seismic specifications. The new face of the city – i.e. what we see today – is an Italian creation, since the Dodecanese was under Italian domination at that time.

The Avenue of the Palms.

The view from the castle of Neratzia is captivating.

bridge which connects Hippocrates' Plane Tree Square with the Kastro is also a product of the period.

The modern city of Kos, built originally around the bay of the same name, forms a semicircle spread over a radius of more than 20 kilometres. With verdant greenery, tall palms, a plethora of trees and flowers, wide roads, special bicycle lanes, parks and squares, buildings with unique architecture, picturesque corners and modern infrastructure, Kos satisfies even the most demanding

Detail with Hippocrates' plane tree from an etching dating from 1822.

visitor who wishes to trace the path of civilization but also enjoy modern, cosmopolitan life.

If we want to take a short walk in the city we should certainly start from the **harbour**. This enclosed but wide bay welcomes dozens of pleasure craft, fishing boats, sponge divers' boats, and cruise boats which organize excursions every day to all destinations in the vicinity. Noisy and cosmopolitan, it throbs with life twenty-four hours a day, since around it the famous **Akti Kountourioti**

bulges with shops, hotels and clubs. All of the eastern wing of the harbour is occupied by the imposing Castle of the Knights. In order to get there, the

Detail from the mosque of the Loggia.

This wonderful Italian building houses the National Tourist Organisation of Greece today.

The characteristic inscription on the fountain in Plane Tree Square.

visitor should walk towards the uniquely beautiful **Avenue of the Palms** and cross the picturesque little stone **bridge**. This avenue was created exactly on the site of the ditch which surrounded the ancient fortress of Kos and was

The eastern gateway of the medieval fortress.

filled with water, joining the harbour with the open sea. Later, the Venetians used the same protective ditch, building their fortress exactly upon the ancient one. The bridge joins the castle with the famous **Hippocrates' Plane Tree Square**. A huge plane tree, with a trunk whose diameter measures around 12 metres, dominates this bustling square; according to tradition the tree was planted by the father of medicine himself, 2,500 years ago, and constitutes the oldest tree in Europe. It was said that Hippocrates himself taught medicine to his students sitting beneath this tree; another tradition tells us that when he came to the

island, the Apostle Paul taught the new religion – Christianity - sitting in its shade. In reality, however, the tree cannot be more than 600 years old. The **fountain** to the north of the plane tree was constructed in its present form during the years of the Turkish occupation, when an ancient sarcophagus was brought there. Later an inscription in Arabic was added to the fountain, which characterizes its water as 'the water of Hippocrates'. The inscription is dated

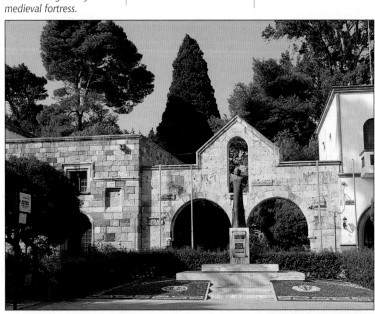

1786, which was the year of the foundation of the nearby **mosque** of Lotzia by the Turkish admiral **Gazi Irli Hasan**. Ancient architectural elements can be seen to have been incorporated into the fabric of the mosque and its typical minaret. After leaving Hippocrates' Plane Tree Square we arrive in **Akti Miaouli** with its sands, ideal for sea bathing. Apart from the beautiful sandy beach along the length of Akti Miaouli, there are a number of the most beautiful buildings in the city, mainly with Italian architecture. The scene is clearly stolen by the magnificent **Government Building** with its characteristic tower and clock. This building, which during

The Defterdar Mosque in Eleftheria Square.

the period of Italian occupation housed the government offices, today houses the Prefecture and the Police Department of Kos. Nearby are the offices of the **archbishopric** and the **eastern gate** of the medieval city; both are among the most imposing sights in the city.

From Akti Miaouli we follow Hippocrates Street which runs at an angle to it, taking a northerly direction. We pass the site of the ancient Agora on our right (we will come back to it later) and continue to **Eleftheria Square**. This most cosmopolitan and bustling square of the city is full of people; they come here for

The interior of the Public Market in Eleftheria Square.

a variety of reasons, a main one being to buy fresh vegetables, fruit and fish from the superb building of the closed **Public Market** with its typical arches, occupying the southern side of the square. Many come to the square to enjoy a cup of coffee in one of its numerous, tasteful and picturesque little cafés; others, by no means few, come here to visit some of the most important landmarks in the city. One of them is the **Defterdar Mosque**, the most imposing Ottoman building in Kos. Constructed in the 18th century, it is excellently preserved and characterized by the minaret and the roofed fountain right next to it. The northern side of the square is taken up by a building with impressive architecture, dating from the Italian occupation; today, it houses the **Archaeological Museum of Kos**, with its impressive mosaics and the famous collection of sculptures which we shall examine below in detail. The so-called '**Forum Gate**' is another landmark in Eleftheria Square, exactly opposite the Defterdar Mosque. This was the medieval entrance to the city of Kos and the ancient Agora - the Forum - from which the gate takes its name. Almost hidden among wonderful bougainvillea there is the "Fonias" (literally 'the killer'), the little balcony-like projection from which the enemies of the city were destroyed when boiling oil was poured on them.

The 'Leschi' building in Eleftheria Square.

The Public Market of Kos in Eleftheria Square.

The Castle of Neratzia

When a visitor enters the harbour at Kos, the castle which covers all of the north-eastern side of the harbour rises up on the left. It is said that during antiquity, the site it occupies was an island which was joined to the mainland of the island by a bridge; this would have been located, probably, in the same position as that of the later bridge over the Street of Palms. It is possible, however, that instead of a little island there was a peninsula here, across the narrow neck of which a defensive ditch had already been dug in antiquity, and over which there was a communicating bridge. This ditch functioned

as a water-filled canal; thus on the one hand it joined the harbour with the open sea, and on the other ensured excellent protection for the castle. The Italian traveller Nicolo de Martoni, a passenger on a boat taking pilgrims to the Holy Places, disembarked in 1394 on Kos and was impressed by the castle of Neratzia. He mentions that it was surrounded on three sides by the sea, and on the fourth by a lagoon or lake. He also notes that the sea passed beneath the bridge of the entrance and communicated with the water in the lake, making the castle impregnable. It is just possible that the word used for lake (limni) referred to the harbour (limani), and that the latter had most probably become silted up and turned into a marsh.
The so-called Castle of Neratzia was built by the Knights of St. John

The frieze with the garlands and figures above the central gateway of the castle.

in the mid-14th century in order to protect the city, which from that time on was known as Neratzia because of the gardens full of citrus tree which existed around the borders of the settlement. To get there, the visitor should go to Hippocrates' Plane Tree Square and then take the

The entrance to the castle via the little bridge.

little bridge which crosses over the Street of Palms. Particular notice should be taken of the Hellenistic frieze decorated with masks and garlands, exactly above the central gateway to the castle. This frieze is especially mentioned by the 18th century traveller E.D.Clarke in his book "Travels in Various Countries of Europe, Asia and Africa" (London, 1814). Proceeding directly beneath it, in the storey of the central gate, we can make out the presence of granite columns which probably came from the early Christian basilica of the Harbour. These, together with the Hellenistic frieze, bear witness to the fact that right from the start, building material for the construction of the castle was of second

or even third-hand usage (inscriptions, architectural components etc). Part of this material was found on the site which had already been inhabited since antiquity, while the rest had been brought from other archaeological sites in the city, and even from the Asklepeion. On entering, we can see that the castle consisted of two fortified courtyards, one internal and one external. The internal courtyard has round towers at each of its four corners; one of them (in the north-west) has been incorporated into the external courtyard. The internal courtyard is clearly smaller than the external one, which instead of towers in its four corners has bastions of large dimension. The two courtyards are separated by a wide ditch and connected by a sloping bridge. In the space between them,

on the north side, there is also a building dating from the time of the Knights' occupation; it is used today as a place of exhibition of sculptures, inscriptions and architectural components. According to the reports of travellers, the internal courtyard was built around the end of the 14th century. The oldest indication of a date inside the castle itself is provided by the coat of arms of the Masters De Lastic (1437-1454) and De Milly (1454-1461) which are set into the wall of the circular tower to the right of

View of the interior of the castle. The internal courtyard with its circular towers is clearly visible.

The interior of the castle with its characteristic courtyards, one internal and one external.

the internal bridge. The external courtyard is of later date; the decision to construct it was taken immediately after the failure of the Knights to defeat the Turks on Rhodes in 1480. Work began in 1495 under the Grand Master D'Aubusson; it was continued under D'Amboise and finished in 1514 by Del Carretto. The coats of arms of all three are set into the walls and the bastions. The external courtyard was built along the lines of a new system based on bastions, with the object of further strengthening the fortress; this system of building forts with bastions instead of high towers was dictated by innovations in warfare tactics, and mainly by the discovery of gunpowder. The south-west semicircular bastion is very imposing with its three rows of canon emplacements; it was built by Grand Master F. del Carretto in 1514, as we can see from the coat of arms in its west wall. Generally, in the external courtyard there is a plethora of

coats of arms set into the walls, which attest to its building over a period of twenty years. When the castle fell into Turkish hands in 1523, entry to it was forbidden not only to Greeks but also to all Europeans, as is witnessed by the 19th century travellers E.D. Clarke and W. Turner. The latter, in his book "Journal of a Tour in the Levant" (London 1820) mentions that the ditch outside the castle did not contain water, that the walls were whitewashed, and that the place was generally in a poor condition. Later, (in 1846) a large part of the castle was destroyed by an explosion of

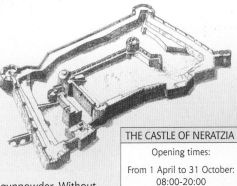

gunpowder. Without doubt, very little work was carried out during the years of the Ottoman occupation and the castle became a picture of decline.

THE CASTLE OF NERATZIA

Opening times:

From 1 April to 31 October: 08:00-20:00

From 1 November to 31 March: 08.30 - 15.00

Closed on Mondays.

Entrance: **3€/2€**

Excavations of the harbour and market place (Agora)

The area which lies between Hippocrates' Plane Tree Square, Akti Miaouli, Eleftheria Square and Akti Kountourioti constitutes the site of the excavations of the harbour and agora. The walled city of the Knights which was once situated here was razed to the ground by the earthquake of 1933, leaving only a

Fragments of columns and other architectural elements at the excavation site of the Agora.

very few sections of the walls standing, as well as the eastern gate (Hippocrates Street) and the Forum Gate (opposite the Defterdar Mosque). Thus an opportunity arose to uncover an archaeological site of huge importance which during ancient times was situated outside the walls of the city. The remains of the structures visible today date mainly from the 4th and 3rd centuries BC, and from the 5th and 6th centuries AD. The latest buildings - of the early Christian era - were constructed exactly on top of the ancient ones which had apparently been razed by an earthquake at some point in time.

The Hellenistic City Wall
When the capital of the island was moved to its north-east tip in 366 BC, the new city was fortified with walls

Part of the Hellenistic wall of the city.

which included towers and gates and were constructed of bulky stone blocks; sections of the walls have been preserved at various locations in the city, to the height of four courses. Part of the north side of the city wall which followed the curving shoreline of the harbour has been discovered in the eastern archaeological zone. An earthquake in 142 BC destroyed the wall almost completely, and it was never rebuilt. The harbour, which had remained outside the city fortifications, was protected by two extensions to the basic wall, one to the east and one to the west.

The Sanctuary of Herakles.

The Sanctuary of Herakles

Of this structure, which must have been very impressive, only the podium and one orthostat are extant; built upon a trapezoidal mound, its dimensions were 12.5 x 9 metres. It was ascribed to Herakles because of the discovery of an inscription and the sculpted head of a lion on the site. The sanctuary must have been built in the 3rd century BC, with the subsequent addition, during the same century, of some separate rooms around it in which there were mosaic floors depicting Orpheus with animals and Herakles at a drinking-party. During the Roman period a stoa was created in front of the sanctuary; it must have been destroyed completely by an earthquake in 469 AD.

The Hellenistic temple.

The Hellenistic Temple

Between the Sanctuary of Herakles and the Stoa of the Harbour there was a small temple of which only the foundation and the lower part have survived. This little temple has been dated to the Hellenistic period but the nature of its dedication remains unknown.

The Sanctuary of Aphrodite

This sanctuary, dedicated to Aphrodite Pandemos (protectoress of love) and Pontia (protectoress of seamen) is dated to the 2nd century BC. It must have been a monumental building, visible from afar to those who approached Kos via the harbour. The sanctuary itself was situated on an artificial mound and was 'twinned', i.e. it contained two Doric temples, each of which had four columns in its façade. Around the temples there were stoas with propylaia in Ionic style on the northern side. The sanctuary was destroyed by the earthquake of 469 AD. Later, baths and an early Christian basilica were built on the same spot. For the building of the latter, material from the ruins of the ancient sanctuary was used.

The Sanctuary of Aphrodite.

The Ancient Agora

As in all the well-organised cities of antiquity, the centre of economic and social life on Kos was to be found in its Agora where, today, two Doric columns are visible. It had a ground plan in the shape of the Greek letter Π, and a north-south orientation. It was about 80 metres in width and its length, as far as can be ascertained from recent excavations, must have exceeded 300 metres. According to some researchers, the southern part of the Agora may well have extended as far as the area of the Altar of Dionysos. The Agora abutted the northern wall of the city, its wall constituting that part of the northern fortification wall. On its other three sides it was enclosed by its own wall, with an encircling roadway on the outside. The Agora contained an internal court with stoas of Doric columns which were fluted only to two-thirds of their height. Behind the stoas there were shops. During the 2nd century BC the internal court was paved with square marble slabs. In Roman times, the earthquake of 142 AD razed the walls on the northern side, at the place where a monumental entrance with three arches and a large stairway leading to the harbour area had been constructed.

The Stoa of the Harbour and the Basilica

The stoa of the harbour is located north-east of the archaeological site of the Agora and south of Hippocrates' Plane Tree Square. The date of its original construction is placed in the 4th or at the beginning of the 3rd century BC and it is the oldest building in the harbour area. Changes were made to it, however, during the 3rd century AD, as is apparent from the remains found between the foundation walls of the later basilica of the 5th century AD. Today,

The restored columns of the ancient market-place.

the visitor can admire the 5 reconstructed Corinthian marble capitals which, during the Roman period, replaced the older ones. During the same period, the rectangular areas formed behind the stoa were covered over with plaster. The stoa, like all the buildings in the vicinity, was destroyed by the earthquake in 469 AD. Amongst the ruins was found the well-known 'table-leg' (table support) dating from the 2nd century BC, depicting Marsyas hanging and awaiting his punishment from Apollo. During the early Christian period (5th and 6th centuries AD) a tripartite basilica with a cruciform

The stoa of the harbour and the early Christian basilica.

baptistery was built on the site of the harbour stoa (Basilica of the Harbour or Land). It must have been the largest basilica on the island, measuring 72 x 23 metres, and was constructed using ancient building material from the structure which had stood on the same spot in antiquity.

The basilica had a rectangular narthex in the west, and an atrium. To the south of it was the baptistery complex which was dedicated to St. John the Baptist. Of the basilica, a section of the stairway which led to the narthex has survived.

The Western Archaeological Zone

This is situated in the south-west of the city, in the area between Gregorios V Street, Megas Alexandros Street, Tsaldaris Street and Peisander Street. This widest of the archaeological sites with its impressive monuments is excellently preserved due to the fact that the area in question was deserted for a number of years, without any building activity taking place there. It contains mainly important public buildings of the Hellenistic and Roman periods.

Via Cardo – Via Decumana

To visit the western archaeological zone, we follow the two central arterial roads of antiquity, the Via Cardo and Via Decumana (as they were named by the Italian archaeologists) for most of the way.

The Via Decumana.

The Via Cardo (meaning 'axis') is paved with large irregular slabs and crosses the archaeological site in a north-south direction; it is 160 metres long and apparently led to the harbour. It is dated to the 3rd century AD and an advanced drainage

The Via Cardo.

system with culverts has been discovered beneath it. The Via Decumana ('great road') follows an east-west orientation and runs almost parallel with the modern Grigorios V Street; it joins the Via Cardo at a right angle. This road, which was built upon the earlier Hellenistic road, contained stoas and measured 30 metres in width.

The Gymnasion and the 'Xystos Dromos'

The impressive columns which greet the visitor in the southern part of the western zone belong to the so-called 'xystos dromos' which constituted part of the Hellenistic gymnasium. The 'xystos dromos' was a roofed-over area where athletic contests took place during the winter months. The name is taken from the practice of the athletes, after their participation in the contests, of 'scraping' their bodies with a special instrument called a strigil, in order to remove oil. The marble columns are in Doric style and unfluted in their lower halves. In all, the building had 81 columns of which only 17 have been restored. The 'xystos dromos' was part of the western gymnasium, the only one of the three gymnasia on Kos dating from the Hellenistic period to have undergone reconstruction. It was rectangular in shape and had an internal peristyle court with Doric columns. In

The restored columns of the Gymnasion.

addition to the 'xystos dromos' there was a road with a width of one 'stadion' around the gymnasium. There were also other structures, such as changing-rooms and memorial monuments. Changes were made to the western gymnasium during the Roman period; a plunge-pool was added, so that the athletes could bathe.

The Ancient Stadium

To the north of the Gymnasion, at the crossroads of modern Megas Alexandros and 31st March Streets, there was the stadium which was largely built in the 4th century BC. Additions, such as the western sector of benches for seating, were made during the Roman period. The stadium was rectangular and measured 180 x 30 metres; all that remains of it is the starting-post, dating from the 2nd century BC and situated beside the little church of St. Anna, and three tiers of stone benches at the southern end.

The Western Baths

To the south-east of the Gymnasium there lies the complex of the western baths, built by the Romans in the 3rd century AD on the ruins of an earlier building. The baths comprise a trapezoidal building with a central, arched meeting-hall, part of which is preserved today. The frigidarium, or cold bath, is preserved in the southern part of the building, while in the centre there was the hot bath (caldarium) with arches and a domed roof. The baths were destroyed by the earthquake of 469 AD and later – in the 5th century AD – the early Christian basilica and baptistery were built upon their ruins.

Building with the mosaic of the "Judgment of Paris"
A large hall with an impressive mosaic floor dating from the 2nd-

A section of the mosaic which has the Judgment of Paris as its central theme.

early 3rd century AD has been discovered to the north of the western baths. This floor, which is probably the largest found on the whole island, depicts a number of scenes, such as those of hunting, the nine Muses with Apollo, and of course the wonderful representation of the Judgment of Paris.

The Nymphaeum or Forica

Although it is called the Nymphaeum, this is simply the Roman public lavatory which was built in the 3rd century AD opposite the western baths and is connected with them. As it is a wonderful architectural edifice, researchers thought it was a sanctuary of the nymphs, and erroneously designated it a Nymphaeum. The building has a square ground plan and contained a peristyle central court. Four Ionic columns on the northern side, four on the southern and five on the eastern side supported arches and formed stoas. The western side comprises a wall with niches and water tanks at ground level. The floor of the internal court is decorated with mosaics which have geometric designs and there is a spring in the middle. The building did not survive the earthquake of 469 AD but it has been possible to reconstruct it almost completely today,

The interior of the so-called 'Nymphaion'.

The reconstructed doorway of the early Christian basilica.

due to the fact that its components were found collected altogether in a lime kiln in the vicinity.

The Early Christian Basilicas

As already indicated, the earthquake of 469 AD destroyed the complex of the western baths. Later, in the early Christian era, two basilicas and a baptistery were built on the same site. One tripartite basilica (the northern church) with a semicircular internal apse (externally three-sided) on the eastern side of the middle aisle, was built on the site of the Roman frigidarium (cold bath). The ground-plan of the basilica appears to have been rectangular and to have measured 16.5 x 16.15 metres. The other basilica (the southern church) was built on the site of the caldarium (hot bath); unfortunately its ground-plan cannot be discerned on the basis of the extant remains. South of this church the existence of a baptistery has come to light, with a forecourt, monumental entrance with a marble door-surround, and numerous mosaic floors.

The House of Europa

The famous House of Europa is situated in the south-west of the western archaeological zone, at the point where the Via Decumana and Via Cardo intersect; the house spreads over almost a whole rectangular block. It is named after the wonderful mosaic floor of one of its rooms, which depicts the well-known myth of the abduction of Europa by Zeus; Europa, naked, is being transported across the sea from Phoenicia clinging to the neck of the bull, which is none other than Zeus in disguise.

The 'Abduction of Europa' in the famous mosaic from the house of the same name.

The House of Europa.

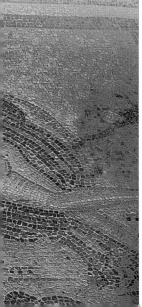

The scene is enhanced by a dolphin and a figure with a torch, most probably representing Eros. Equally impressive mosaics decorate the other rooms of the house, with subject-matter taken from the realms of nature and the world of mythology. The house was built in the 2nd century AD on the site of an earlier Hellenistic house and had an internal peristyle court. It was decorated with statues which are housed today in the Archaeological Museum of Kos.

The Odeion

The Italian archaeologist Laurenzi discovered the Odeion in 1929 at the southern end of the western archaeological zone, on the side opposite Grigorios V Street. It is still the venue for a number of cultural events today. In its little theatre dating from the 2nd century AD, the first 9 steps of the lower landing, all marble-clad, constitute an impressive sight. The second landing has limestone tiers, one left and one right, and at the ends of the tiers there are two stairways with 18 steps, to enable theatre-goers to move around.

View of the Odeion from the point of access.

The Odeion.

The floor of the semicircular orchestra was decorated in opus sectile technique, i.e. with little pieces of marble arranged to form geometric designs. Three openings in the stage led to a room behind. In the places below the tiers many statues have been found, among them the famous one of Hippocrates which can be seen today in the Archaeological Museum of Kos.

The Roman House (Casa Romana)

The excellence, size and impressive decoration of this Roman house led its excavator, the Italian archaeologist L. Laurenzi, to name it the 'Casa Romana'. The house is situated at the south-east end of the western archaeological zone, exactly south of the Via Decumana, and it covers an area of 2,400 square metres which corresponds to a whole rectangular block (insula) of the ancient city. In addition to the majestic architecture of the building with its 40 rooms, what impresses the observer most is the rich decoration of the spaces with mosaic floors, the marble cladding of the walls, and the marble statues. A house already existed at this spot in the Hellenistic period;

this fact is evidenced by the nature of the fabric of the wall on the north side of the building. The dwelling was reconstructed after the earthquake of 142 AD, while further modifications were made in the 3rd century AD, with the enrichment of the decoration and additions to the mosaics. As already mentioned, the house comprised more than 40 rooms, two peristyle courts and an atrium. The atrium (XV) is characterised by the little ornamental pool and the mosaic depicting a fight between animals. Room XVII is associated with this atrium and must have constituted a reception room. Its main feature is the floor of opus sectile and the mosaic with the fish which can be seen today in the Archaeological Museum. The peristyle hall XVIII is enhanced by a little pool, the sides of which are decorated by mosaics, and there are also wall-paintings and little statues. The floor mosaic has Nereids riding on a hippocamp as its central theme, surrounded by panthers and dolphins; in general, the decoration of this peristyle hall has 'wet elements' as its main subject-matter. In peristyle hall

Mosaic from the Casa Romana.

XXVIII the colonnade surrounds the garden with its little pool and six decorative statues. Into this luxurious place with its marble cladding on the walls, there opened other magnificent rooms with marble floors decorated with geometric designs, and representations of a tiger, panther etc. These probably served as reception rooms, and were necessary to emphasize the wealth of the owner. The 'mens'

Mosaic with a representation of fishes from the Casa Romana. (Archaeological Museum of Kos).

quarters' faced onto this area and connected with the superb large hall known as the 'triclinium' (XXXI), decorated with opus sectile on the floor and

walls. The little room XXXIV immediately next to the 'triclinium' was decorated with an impressive mosaic floor depicting a panther.

The Altar of Dionysos

Almost opposite the Casa Romana, in the north-east of the western archaeological zone and inside the park between Byron Street and St. Nicholas Street, the spades of the Italian archaeologists uncovered the altar of Dionysos during the decade of the 30s. This is a typical Hellenistic altar with an architectural arrangement in the form of a Greek letter Π. Its construction is assigned to the 2nd century BC and it is believed to have been accomplished with funding from the kings of Pergamon during the period in which they were allies of the island. Entrance to the altar was from the western side by means of a ramp. Inside it was the offertory table ('bench') on which there is a sculpted frieze. The latter, which is a work of the 2nd century BC and is housed today in the castle of Neratzia, depicts scenes of the Battle of the Amazons and the Dionysiac entourage. Internally, the sides of the altar to the left and right of the entrance were also decorated in relief, as was the whole of the external façade of the altar. A Doric temple has also been discovered at the same site; this was most probably also dedicated to Dionysos.

The Central Archaeological Zone

This zone begins in the neighbourhoods of the Seraglio and Halvazia and is bordered by the modern 31st March Street, Kolokotronis Street, Peisander Street and Eleftheria Square. Archaeological excavations here have revealed the oldest residential nucleus of Kos, with finds in the area ranging from the Minoan to the Roman period. In addition to the cemetery which has been discovered on the Seraglio Hill in the neighbourhoods mentioned, the existence of a settlement there in the archaic period has been ascertained. A sanctuary dating from the archaic period, its use as a place of worship clearly indicated by the small finds from the excavations, has recently been discovered a short distance away (about 3 kms). The Geometric necropolis contained the graves of 77 children, a number of tombs of adults and a multitude of vessels which are on display today in the Archaeological Museum.

The ancient acropolis of Kos has been discovered on the hill at the intersection of Peisander and Kolokotronis Streets.

The so-called "House of the Bronzes" was discovered in the eastern part of the central archaeological zone; it takes its name from the bronze statuettes of Isis, Aphrodite, Ares and Demeter that were found there.

One of the most important finds from this zone is the mosaic which depicts the arrival of Asklepios on Kos by boat, with Hippocrates seated a short distance off. This mosaic, located today in the Archaeological Museum, was found in one of the Roman houses which were discovered to the south of the church of Ayia Paraskevi.

The famous mosaic depicting the arrival of Asklepios on the island. Archaeological Museum of Kos.

The Archaeological Museum

The archaeological museum of Kos is housed in a building with wonderful architecture of Italian influence, situated in Eleftheria Square exactly opposite the public market. The two-storeyed building with its triple arched entrance comprises a peristyle internal court with three halls around it, which house the collection of sculptures and mosaics. On the upper floor there is a collection of pottery dating from the Geometric to the Hellenistic period, although the latter is not accessible to the public. Also to be found here is the whole prehistoric collection with finds from the Seraglio Hill and the Neolithic cave of Aspri Petra.

On entering the museum we find ourselves in the anteroom where there are cylindrical

The open courtyard of the Archaeological Museum.

and rectangular types of altars and large reliefs and sculptures. From the anteroom the

Group consisting of Dionysos, Pan, and a satyr.

This sculpture, executed with amazing skill, originates from the house with the mosaic of Europa and is dated to the 2nd century AD. It depicts the god Dionysos in a state of drunkenness and trying – with difficulty – to remain upright. For this reason he is supporting himself on a satyr with his right hand and holds a torch (thyrsos) with a vine in his left hand. Above the thrysos, Pan is sitting and playing his pipes, while at the feet of the god and the satyr there are cupids playing with a panther.

impressive atrium or internal peristyle court of the museum is visible; the central exhibit here is the famous mosaic of the 2nd century which covers the floor. It depicts the arrival of Asklepios on the island by boat. Hippocrates is waiting for him on the shore, sitting beside a rock, along with a Koan who is shown standing and welcoming the god. This wonderful floor was brought to light by the archaeologist's spade in 1935, during excavations in the area near the church of Ayia Marina. In the peristyle around the mosaic floor there are some of the more typical sculptures of the museum, such as the group consisting of Dionysos, Pan, and a satyr (2nd century AD), a statue of Artemis ready to loose one of her arrows (2nd century AD), a statue of Hygeia holding a snake (2nd century AD), a statue of a lady of the time of Trajan (2nd century AD), a statue of a young woman, also from the time of Trajan (2nd century AD), and a mosaic depicting fish from the Casa Romana etc.

Statue of Artemis

Artemis, with her intricate hairstyle,and wearing a pleated, short chiton and light cloak which emphasizes the contours of her breast, is shown standing. She is ready to fire an arrow with her right hand, while in her left she holds the quiver. A dog sits at her feet. The statue originates from the house with the mosaic of Europa and dates from the 2nd century AD.

Statue of Hygeia

This statue was found in the house with the mosaic of Europa and is dated to the 2nd century AD. It represents the daughter of Asklepios standing and holding a snake in her right hand; she is feeding it with an egg. At her feet there is the seated figure of a little winged god, probably Eros or Hypnos. The hairstyle and the clothing of the goddess are impressive; she wears the typical light cloak, beneath which the heavy, pleated chiton is visible.

Statues of women

These date from the late Hellenistic period and were found in the vicinity of the Odeion.

To the left, as we look towards the peristyle hall, there is the west room of the museum with exhibits mostly of Hellenistic or Roman date. Amongst them are the statues of women from the Odeion, the funerary stele of an athlete, a large head of Herakles from Kefalos, and a head of Alexander.

Statue of a lady

This is the statue of a mature woman who is shown standing and wearing a heavy, long pleated chiton and a cloak which is wrapped around her whole body, leaving only her throat and the lower part of her arms free. This statue of a serious, reticent woman dates from the time of Trajan (2nd century AD) and comes from the house with the mosaic of Europa.

Head of a woman

Dating from the late Hellenistic period, this head of a woman is of excellent workmanship.

Funerary stele of an athlete

This stele dates from the 3rd century BC and was found in the vicinity of the Roman theatre, near the Classical wall. The young, beardless athlete, standing, is wearing a cloak which leaves the upper part of his body uncovered. He is holding a victory crown and on his chest there is an inscription 'DAID', which probably means 'Daidalos'.

In the north of the west room there is the niche which contains the statue of Hippocrates. Also  located there is an archaic relief with the scene of a symposium (drinking party); it was found on the Seraglio Hill.

Statue of a woman

Found in the Odeion, this statue dates from the late Hellenistic period. This particular type of female statue with a heavy chiton and cloak covering the whole body and the arms is designated 'classicizing', i.e. it is based on sculpted prototypes of the Classical period.

The so-called 'Hippocrates'

This statue, dating from the 4th century BC, was found in the Odeion and 'christened' Hippocrates by workers on the excavation there. It represents a bearded man with a cloak which is wrapped around his body, leaving the right shoulder and the chest uncovered.

Leaving the niche which contains 'Hippocrates' and continuing to the left, we come to the north room of the museum where the display consists mostly of sculptures from the Sanctuary of Demeter at Amani, such as the statues of Demeter, Hades and Persephone and also an inscription of the 4th century BC dedicated to the 'Daughter' (Persephone). The well-known statue of armed

The armed Aphrodite

This marble statue was found in the Casa Romana and dates from the Hellenistic period. Of wonderful workmanship, it depicts the goddess naked, with her cloak left at her feet.

Aphrodite, statues of nymphs, satyrs, Tyche and the Muse Kleio are among others also to be found here.

Lastly, in the east room of the museum, there are works dating mainly from the Roman period. Amongst them are the statues of Hygeia, Hermes, and Artemis of Ephesos. There is also the table-support which depicts the hanging Marsyas who awaits his punishment from Apollo (2nd century BC) etc.

Part of an archaic pediment with a helix.

Statue of Hermes

Statue dating from the 2nd century AD, which was found in the house with the mosaic of Europa. The god is depicted sitting on a rock; he wears a winged cap and sandals, and carries a wand. A light cloak is wrapped around his throat, falls to the side and returns to the front to cover part of his right shoulder. Hermes rests his left hand on the head of a ram which is standing beside him.

THE ASKLEPEION

The Asklepeion

At a distance of scarcely 4 kms, the Sanctuary of Asklepios, the famous Asklepeion, is very near to the city of Kos. Visitors approach it along the road which begins from the city, runs in a south-west direction and passes through the suburb of Platani or Kermetes. There is a mosque here, as the majority of the inhabitants of the suburb are Moslems. This wide, cypress-lined road leads to the archaeological site. The route is level without any uphill stretches, and can be very easily accomplished on a bicycle. As soon as

Asklepios, the god of therapeutics, was the son of Apollo and the nymph Koronis. When Apollo learned that Koronis, who was already pregnant with Asklepios, intended to marry another, he brought about her demise. He managed, however, to acquire the unborn child and gave it to the centaur Cheiron on Pelion, to be brought up. The god was taught medicine by the wise centaur and managed to gain more renown than his teacher. It was actually said that when he came to the point of being able to raise the dead, Zeus punished him by hurling a thunderbolt. All of the daughters of Asklepios (Hygeia, Iaso, Akeso, Panacaea and Ipione) and his two sons (Machaonas and Podaleirios) were closely connected with medicine.

we approach the site it becomes apparent that it spreads over a little hill and for this reason is arranged in three terraces at specific levels, to enable the building of the various structures which make up the Sanctuary. There is a panoramic view from the hill; the vista that unfolds before the eyes of the visitor takes in not only the endless plain of Kos but also the coastline of Asia Minor. It is probable that the choice of this location

In addition to Asklepios, the Asklepeion of Kos was closely connected with **Hippocrates** who laid the foundations of medical science, contributing decisively to the spread of the fame of the sanatorium. He was born on the island in 460 BC and died in Thessaly around 377 BC.

for the construction of the Asklepeion, i.e. the therapeutic centre of the epoch, was not due to chance, but conditioned by the physical beauty of the area, the clean air and the dense forest which surrounded the site. By the same token, it is not by chance that the copse in question was already a sacred site, dedicated to Apollo

Kyparissios and, as evidenced by Pausanias, that no murder and no birth was permitted there. At the same time, the sanatorium enjoyed an inexhaustible supply of clean, hot water from the springs around it, for example that of Vourrina. This spring is situated in the foothills of Mount Dikaios to the south-east of the archaeological site and still supplies the city of Kos with water today. Its waters had therapeutic properties by reason of their high content of iron and sulphur. The spring, which according to Theocritos burst forth when the mythical king of Kos, Halkonas, struck his foot on the rock, is located in the depths of a dark tunnel which is vaulted and built of polygonal stones; in the upper part there is an opening for ventilation and light. The structure

dates from the Hellenistic period. The Asklepeion of Kos and all the Asklepeia everywhere else in Greece were originally founded to honour the great contribution of Asklepios to medicine. Later, they developed into medical centres and for this reason were all built close to nature, in idyllic locations suited to the treatment of the sick. It is calculated that there were around 300 Asklepeia in ancient Greece; of these the most important were in Trikki (Thessaly), Epidauros, Kos, Athens and Leros. As the Asklepeia were at first religious sanctuaries, medicine was originally practised by the priests themselves. They placed the sick under a multitude of

The first terrace of the archaeological site.

treatments and cures until the appearance of Hippocrates, who laid the foundations of medical science. It is said that the worship of Asklepios was introduced on Kos by the Thessalians or the Epidaurians; according to one view the latter established the first Asklepeion on the island. The foundation, which included the altar and the little Ionic temple on the second terrace-level, is ascribed to the 4th century BC, contemporary with the founding of the city of Kos. Its Panhellenic reputation is due both to the 'Asklepiades' – physicians who were descendants of Asklepios and initiates who practised the very ancient medicine of Asklepios, and to Hippocrates who was

also a descendant of the same, but advanced medicine from the level of superstition to that of a science. The foundation of the school of medicine, the proclamation of sacred immunity and the institution of the Great Asklepeia also contributed decisively to the spread of the fame of the sanctuary and dictated the need for the extension of the building structures and renovations during the 2nd century BC. At that time, the great temple on the second terrace-level was constructed and the altar rebuilt. Later, during the 1st century AD, the Lavatory and the Temple of Xenophon were added, and later on still the Temple of Apollo (in Corinthian style), and

the baths of the 3rd century AD. Later, the church of Panayia of Tarsus was built on the site of the temple; nothing survives of the church except for one capital dating from the early Christian era. During the period of domination by the Knights the Asklepeion suffered from continuous denudation of its architectural components, which were used as building material in the medieval castle. The Asklepeion was discovered by the German archaeologist **Rudolf Herzog** during excavations which he carried out at the beginning of the 20th century on the basis of clues provided by the Koan historical researcher **Iakovos Zaraftis**. The latter

identified its exact location on the basis of the large number of inscriptions and architectural fragments which existed in the area, as well as the correlation of the site with the springs of Vourinna and Kokkinonero. Through his persistence he managed to persuade the German archaeologist, who had hitherto been unsuccessful in locating the site, to dig in that particular area. The research was fruitful and continued until 1904; during the period many dozens of valuable objects were taken away to Berlin via Constantinople. Excavations ceased after 1904 and were resumed after the earthquake of 1933 by the Italian archaeologists Laurenzi and Morricone. They proceeded to carry out renovation work, restoring the site and giving it its appearance today.

As has already been mentioned, the archaeological site follows the slope of the hill, which has a height of 100 metres. It is divided into three terrace-levels, which are adjoining and interconnected by steps. On arrival, the visitor comes to the monumental propylon dating from the 3rd century BC and the imposing stairway with 24 steps **(1)**. This leads to the first terrace which contains a stoa in the shape of the Greek letter Π. Behind this stoa, which closes off the terrace on the north, east and west sides, there are the rooms **(2)** where the sick and worshippers at the sanctuary were accommodated. To the north-east of the stoa were the baths **(3)** used for treatments with thermal waters, and in the south-west the lavatories **(4)**.

On the southern side of the terrace there was a retaining wall in which there was a row of fountains **(5)**, niches for statues **(6)**, a little shrine dedicated to Asklepios and his daughters Hygeia and Ipione by the famous Coan physician Gaius Sterinius Xenophon **(7)**, and a monumental stairway with 30 steps **(8)** which led up to the middle terrace. According to one

The second terrace of the Asklepeion. From the right: the Temple of Apollo, the altar and the Temple of Asklepios.

Niches and statues on the first terrace of the site.

The monumental stairway which leads to the second terrace.

view, there was a small temple on the first terrace dedicated to Aphrodite, which contained Praxiteles' masterpiece, the statue of the goddess. Almost in the centre of the

second terrace there was the oldest building of the sanctuary which dated from the 4th century BC. This was the Hellenistic altar of Apollo Kyparissios or Asklepios **(9)**, the sculpted decoration of which is thought to have been the work of the sons of Praxiteles. Unfortunately, only scant fragments of this decoration have survived. To the west of the altar lay the temple of Asklepios **(10)**, dating from the 3rd century BC, which was 'two-columned in aspect', i.e. in its façade a stoa was formed by two columns between the lintels. Two of its Ionic columns have been restored and can be seen today in their original position. The temple consisted only of a porch (pronaos) and a central hall (cella), where there was a pit which, with the aid of inscriptions, has been identified as

the 'treasury' of the temple, i.e. the place where the money and votive objects offered to the god by the sick were kept. The 'abaton' or 'place of sleeping', a building with a four-columned Doric vestibule **(11)** which probably comprised a complex of rooms for the priesthood, has been discovered to the south of the temple of Asklepios. To the west of the altar there was a Corinthian 'kiosk' (peripteros) temple of the Roman period **(12)** dedicated to Apollo, father of Asklepios and protector of the Sanctuary before the worship of the god of medicine was introduced. Today, seven of the Corinthian columns and the base of one other have been restored and are in their original positions. The

The Corinthian temple of Apollo.

THE ASKLEPEION

LOWER TERRACE
1. Entrance stairway (24 steps)
2. Rooms for the sick
3. Baths
4. Lavatories
5. Fountains
6. Niches for statues
7. Little temple of
   Asklepios
8. Stairway to the middle
   terrace

SECOND TERRACE
9. Altar to Asklepios
10. Temple of Asklepios
11. Rooms of the
    priesthood
12. Temple of Apollo
13. Hall of dedications
14. Rostrum
15. Monumental stairway

THIRD TERRACE
16. Stoa
17. Doric temple of Asklepios

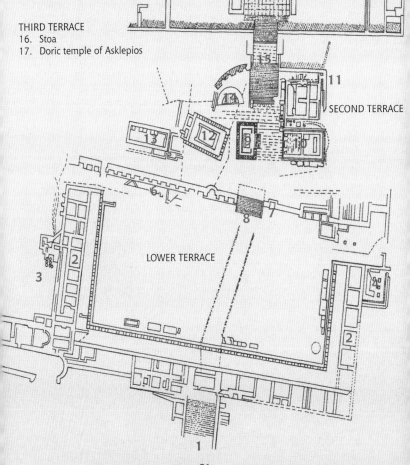

The Temple of Asklepios.

remains in a rectangular area **(13)** to the east of the temple of Apollo belong to a stoa-like room which was used to house votive objects. To the south of the same temple a semicircular dais can be seen **(14)**; this was where the priesthood and physicians from the sanatorium met together to confer. Another monumental stairway, this time with 60 steps **(15)**, led up to the third terrace which measures 80 x 100 metres and was enclosed on the south, east and west sides by a stoa in the shape of the Greek letter Π **(16)**, of which only very few parts have survived. There were rooms for the sick and for worshippers at the sanctuary at the back of the stoa, while at its southern edge a stairway connected the third terrace with the sacred grove. The large Doric temple of Asklepios, dating from the 2nd century BC, dominated the centre of the terrace **(17)**. This temple, which was identical to that of Asklepios in Epidauros, was of 'kiosk' (peripteros) type and surrounded by 104 columns. At a later date this ancient temple was converted into a Christian church, that of Panayia of Tarsus, a name which some believe means the 'Virgin of the Grove'.

The Doric temple of Asklepios.

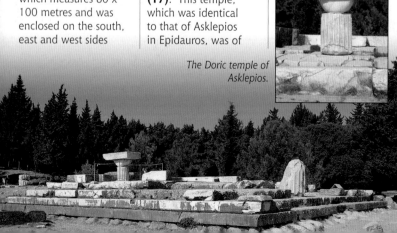

EXCURSIONS
AROUND THE ISLAND

Kos - Psalidi - Ayios Fokas - Therma

We begin from the city of Kos and proceed in a south-easterly direction, in order to visit the more easterly part of the island. A little outside the city and at a distance of only

Christian building of the 4th century. There are various buildings around it and the baptistery was situated in the south-west. Both the basilica and the baptistery were destroyed by the earthquake which struck the island around 553/4 AD. We continue on our way and at a distance of 4 kilometres come to the seaside resort of **Psalidi** with its endless sandy beach, modern tourist infrastructure, luxury

a pleasant ride without inclines, beneath the lines of trees and almost next to the sea. After Psalidi we continue eastwards and follow the road which approaches the two peninsulas, **Louros** and

The early Christian basilica of Ayios Gabriel.

2 kilometres, in the place called 'Psalidi', we come to the ruins of the **Early Christian Basilica of Ayios Gabriel**, situated on the right. This church was tripartite with a narthex and a dome, and built in the 6th century AD on the site of an older

hotels and also the camping site of Kos. It is worth mentioning that the route here from the city of Kos can best be accomplished by bicycle. The special cyclists' lane which runs parallel to the main road assures

The beach and the place of healing waters at Therma.

Ayios Fokas. The latter is craggy and constitutes the eastern end of the only mountain on Kos, Mount Dikaios. The locality probably took its name from one of the Byzantine churches which existed there. After a total excursion of around 12 kilometres we come to **Therma**, a little bay with sulphurous thermal waters. On the little beach, with its umbrellas and refreshment kiosk, visitors can take a warm, therapeutic bath, which is ideal for rheumatic and gynaecological conditions.

The beach at Therma.

Kos - Zipari - Asfendiou - Tingaki - Alykes

With the aim of getting to know the mountainous part of Kos, we take the central arterial road in a south-westerly direction from the city. We pass the turn-off for Platani and the Asklepeion and after 8 kilometres come to one of the settlements of the hinterland, Zipari, which is located in a huge area of plain. Two of the most important early Christian basilicas of

the island, those of St. Paul and Kapamas, are worthy of a visit here. They were discovered during archaeological excavations carried out in 1935 under the supervision of the archaeologist Anastasios Orlandos. **The basilica of Ayios**

east section there is the baptistery; its walling is of rough stone, preserved almost to its original height. The floor was paved with white slabs, while in the middle there was a font in the shape of a cross. The basilica and baptistery date from

The early Christian basilica in the place called Kapamas.

Pavlos is situated around 200 metres east of the village and to the south of the main road. A dirt track leads us to the ruins of this early Christian basilica which was tripartite and wooden roofed, and of considerable dimensions (21.6 x 15 metres). In the south-

the 5th century AD and must have been destroyed around the mid-6th century. We return to Zipari and follow the road to Asfendiou, north of the village. To the right of the road, in the place called '**Kapamas**', there are the remains of a

The early Christian basilica of Ayios Pavlos.

The wooded Mount Dikaios.

tripartite basilica whose dimensions measured 17 x 16.4 metres. In the south-east corner of the basilica the remains of a baptistery are visible which was square in shape on the outside and circular on the inside. At its centre there is a large cruciform font, and a smaller one in each of two corners (in the south-west and north-west). The basilica and baptistery must have been built after 469 and destroyed around 553/4. We leave Zipari and continue on the road which now ascends towards Mount Dikaios, and after 5 kilometres arrive at the picturesque mountain village of **Asfendiou**. Amidst a verdant, forested area with gushing waters and a wonderful view out over the plain of Kos,

there is a group of small villages: **Evangelistria**, Asomatos, Lagoudi, Zia and Ayios Demetrios. In these clean and well-looked after little hamlets, with their beautiful, flower-filled courtyards, the visitor may stop to admire the view, take a cup of coffee or even stay over in one of the attractive and modern tourist facilities. Ascending the road, we come first to Evangelistria, named after the church which dominates the central square. From the latter,

a dirt track leads to the villages of Ayios Yeoryios and Ayios Demetrios, which are almost deserted. In the case of Ayios Demetrios or Haïhoutes, there is witness to the fact that there were 30 houses there around the middle of the 19th century, arranged around a spring. Another road out of Evangelistria leads

The Church of Evangelistria in the central square of the village of the same name.

to Lagoudi with its church of St. John the Theologian. We follow the asphalt road and ascend still further to beautiful **Zia**, clinging to the lower slopes of the mountain. Picturesque, very green, with an uninterrupted view, lively during the summer months, tranquil during the winter, with tastefully appointed houses and shops, it is an ideal resort both in summer and winter. Traditional weaving and pottery are to be found here; 'spoon sweets', aromatic herbs and the famous local beverage made of cinnamon all impart a certain colour to this place and invite you to try them. It is worth paying a visit to **Panayia Kouvoukliani or the Monastery of Spondi**, a monastery in the mountains around the village, which according to tradition was founded in the 11th century by Hosios Christodoulos; it can be reached through the village. Visitors can admire the beautiful church which is a simple variant of the cruciform domed type. There are alcoves inside the eastern wall, and four columns

Bustling Zia surprises with picturesque snapshots…

support the dome and the octagonal internal vault. The church has suffered many architectural additions and alterations over the course of time, therefore it is impossible to assign it an exact date. After

The majestic church of the Panayia of Kouvoukliani.

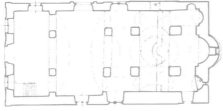

The view from the café outside the church of the Panayia of Kouvoukliani is captivating.

your visit, you can relax in the café next door, which has an endless view towards the north and the north-eastern side of Kos, as well as to the islands opposite, Pserimos and Kalymnos. Another monastery, which according to tradition was built by the Koan monk Arsenios Skinouris in 1079, is **Moni Sotiros or Dikaiou Christou** on the peak of the mountain. It has a small vaulted-roofed church with a little dome, measuring 10 x 5.5 metres, which according to some authorities does not date from the 11th century but from the post-Byzantine period. The possibility cannot be excluded

that the church we see today was built on the site of an older one. The remains of three monks' cells are visible to the south-west of the church and probably belonged to the old ecclesiastical complex which had the character of a hermitage rather than that of a monastery. There are no words to describe the majestic view from the top of Mount Dikaios, which constitutes a panoramic vista not only towards Kos but also over the neighbouring islands. After our beautiful excursion into the mountainous area of the island and the picturesque villages of Asfendiou, we descend the mountain in a northwards direction;

our destination is the seaside settlement of **Tingaki**, which also belongs to the community of Asfendiou. After another 6.5 kilometres, we come to our destination, a resort with a wonderful sandy beach, many tourist facilities, modern hotels, sea sports and a vibrant night life. If the bustling atmosphere of the place does not attract, it is worth proceeding westwards and visiting **Alykes**, about 1 kilometre distant. At this sea lagoon of unique physical beauty, where salt has been collected since early times, we can enjoy the peace and quiet of a summer sunset.

Sunset at Alikes.

Kos - Linopotis - Pyli - Marmari

Starting from the city of Kos, we follow the main arterial road in a south-westerly direction. Beyond the crossroads for Platani and Zipari, and after a distance of 13 kilometres, we come to the locality of **Linopotis**; this huge area of plain is provided with water by the spring called Limni, which is situated in idyllic surroundings. In 1936, in the place called 'Fouskoma', the remains of an agricultural villa were discovered. After our visit to Linopotis we turn left towards the south and 5 kilometres further on come to

Palio Pyli in the foothills of Mount Dikaios, in the area called Amani today. The inhabitants of this silent village were forced to abandon it in 1830 after an epidemic. They moved further north and founded Pyli, which we shall visit later. It is worth going to look at the more mountainous part of the settlement with the remains of the castle and the **Monastery of Theotokos Kastriani**. The earliest information we have about the castle assigns it to the middle of the Byzantine period and connects it with the life of the founder of the Monastery of Patmos, Hosios Christodoulos. According to evidence, Emperor Alexios I Komninos bestowed the castle and the area of Pyli on the latter in 1085. Christodoulos founded the Monastery of the Theotokos (Mother of Christ)

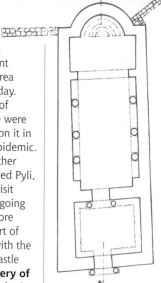

Façade of the church of Panayia of Kastriani.

and presented it to the Byzantine state in exchange for the Monastery of Patmos, intending to retreat from the bustling life of Kos. The fortification at Pyli, which is mentioned by all the travellers of the 15th and 16th centuries, was an important place of refuge for the population throughout the period of the Knights' occupation,

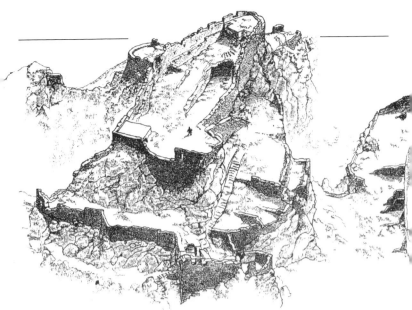

and when the Order decided to evacuate the island and transfer the population to Rhodes, the castle at Pyli was the only place to remain manned and operational. Although the castle played an important role during the years of the Turkish occupation, the epidemic in 1830 forced the population to leave and move to Neo Pyli and Asfendiou. In the pass which is formed between the steep hill with the fort and the mountain next to it, there is the

The fortified hill with the castle at Palio Pyli.

medieval settlement of Palaio Pyli, while traces of habitation during antiquity (pottery of the Bronze Age and parts of cyclopean walls) have been located on the north-west sides of the castle. It cannot be said with certainty that the Mycenaean wall which has come to light provides evidence of the existence of a fortification during antiquity. It is only certain that, at the end of the 11th and beginning of the 12th

centuries AD, there was a castle which, according to Hosios Christodoulos, was built by him in an area that had hitherto been deserted. Today, the visitor can easily discern several of the building phases and more than one courtyard of the **castle**. The central gate, the interior of which is designed as a cruciform church, belongs without doubt to the first building phase. It bears witness to the fact

that there were clear architectural influences from Constantinople during the development of the castle. Whatever its connection may have been with the capital, the fort continued to be occupied after it was captured by the Franks. Without doubt, the most important phase of occupation of the castle was that during the period of the Knights of St. John, from the mid-14th century until 1522, when it constituted the most important fortification on the island. Architectural elements aimed at the reinforcement of its defenses - namely slits for archers and sharply pointed arches - can be clearly seen. The castle continued to be inhabited even after the island was captured by the Ottomans, who also made architectural alterations; thus it always retained its defensive character. The church of the Monastery of **Theotokos Kastriani** near the castle of Pyli was built by Hosios Christodoulos in the 11th century on the ruins of an older, early Christian church. Although it is mentioned in written sources as an important church, both its architecture as a single-aisled domed structure and its decoration are characterised by superb simplicity, in contrast to the main gate of the castle. This contrast, together with the majestic architecture of the latter, have led a number of experts to the conclusion that the Gate was not the work of Christodoulos. Today, apart from the monastery church, remains of the monks' cells and the courtyard of the monastery can be seen to the north-east of the settlement of Pyli.

There are two more Byzantine churches of the 11th and 12th centuries with important frescoes in the area of Pyli, west of the castle and on the lower slopes of the same hill. These are the churches of **Ayii**

Asomati and **Ayios Antonios**.

About 3 kilometres north-west of Palaio Pyli there is the new village of Pyli, founded after the old one was abandoned in 1830. Along the way from Palaio Pyli and after the village of Amani, there extends an endless, fertile plain watered by the lake of Linopotis. This is an area of rich agricultural production, including the most extensive area of tomato cultivation on the island. We should note here that Kos is one of the most important producers of tomatoes in Greece, and it is no coincidence that the sweet little tomatoes are one of the traditional delicacies of the island. The fertility of the area provides the reason for the existence here in antiquity of a sanctuary dedicated to Demeter and the Daughter (Persephone), which has been discovered in the place called Kyparissi at the village of Amani. The ritual of the 'thalysia' (the offering of the first fruits of the harvest) was celebrated here, to give thanks for the fertility of the soil and the harvest. Sculptures from the sanctuary are housed in the museum of Kos. In the modern **village of Pyli** there are two archaeological sights which are definitely worth a visit: the tomb of Harmylos and the spring of Harmylia. **The tomb of Harmylos** is located in the upper part of the village next to the little church of Timios Stavros. This monument dates from the Hellenistic period and is dedicated to Harmylos, the mythical king of Kos, or to the progenitor of a wealthy and aristocratic family from Kos. It is probable that the 'Harmylii' were a family of landowners who built the family tomb on their property. The underground chambered tomb 'of Harmylos' is preserved;

Endless, fertile expanses in the island interior.

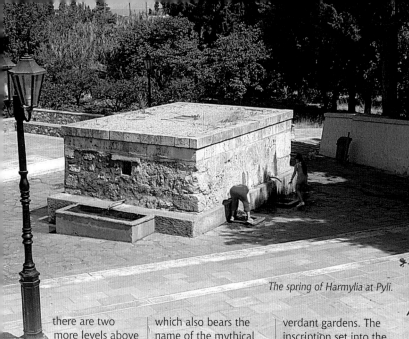

The spring of Harmylia at Pyli.

there are two more levels above it, with hewn crypts for the dead. The spring of **Harmylia**, which also bears the name of the mythical king or hero, is situated within the village and provides water for its verdant gardens. The inscription set into the fabric of the structure is dated 1592, apparently the year in which renovation work was carried out on it.

We leave Pyli and proceed northwards. After about 2 kilometres we come to Linopotis and the main arterial road of the island. We turn left and a little further on, turn right towards **Marmari**. At this seaside village, which has a wonderful beach 2 kilometres in length, there is every kind of up-to-date facility for a pleasant holiday - excellent hotels, rooms, clubs, and of course vibrant night life, are to be found here.

The legendary tomb of Harmylos at Pyli.

Kos - Antimahia - Kardamaina - (Alasarna) - Mastihari

With the city of Kos as our point of departure, we take the main road towards the south-west of the island. After passing the crossroads with turn-offs for Platani/Asklepeion, Zipari and Linopotis, we come to **Antimahia** which is 22.5 kilometres away; this was the centre of the ancient 'deme' of the Antimahides. It is a large area, both in terms of size and population, and organised into settlement

Folk exhibits in the traditional house at Antimahia.

neighbourhoods; there is rich production from agriculture and animal-keeping here. The island airport, named after Hippocrates, is also located here.

A characteristic of the region is its close connection with folk traditions, which are maintained and expressed in many ways in the everyday life of its inhabitants. A particular example is that of the relationship of the local people with traditional music; the lyricist, song-writer, and maker of musical instruments are typical inhabitants. There is a

lot of sightseeing to be done in Antimahia: traditional houses, the windmill, the churches of Ayios Yeoryios Dromikos,

The traditional Antimahian house, a typical example of folk architecture, is located on the central square and represents a traditional dwelling of the beginning of the 20th centre. The visitor can see the barn containing agricultural implements, a weaving loom, traditional costumes for men and women, the stand in which the stamna (pottery water vessel) was placed in the courtyard, and even the hen-coop and the little stall for the pig. Exactly opposite the house there is 'the priest's mill', also a representative example of the architecture at the beginning of the 20th century.

The Priest's Mill at Antimahia.

location, capable of exercising control over all the movement in the interior of the island, from the northern to the southern tip. Although Antimahia itself is mentioned in documents dating from the Byzantine period, the first reference to a **castle** there dates from the period after the capture of the island by the Knights of St. John in 1337. In particular it is mentioned that the castle was built by the Master Helion de Villeneuve, which places its foundation between 1337 when the Knights first arrived, and 1346 (the date of his death). Strength and efficient organisation led it to hold out against the Turkish incursions of the 15th and 16th centuries, among them the great siege of 1457. For 23 days, with a force of 16,000 men, the Turks attempted without success to take the castle and subsequently withdrew,

The central gateway of the castle of Antimahia.

The D'Aubusson coat of arms above the central gateway.

Ayios Yeoryios Makris, and Ayia Marina, and of course, the famous castle of Antimahia. Three kilometres outside the village, on the road towards Kardamaina, we come to the castle in its majestic setting.

There is actually a plain here in the centre of the island, from which there is an endless view out over the strait between Kos and Nisyros. Although not a natural fortification, due to its position at the exact centre of the island it constitutes an excellent strategic

View of the castle of Antimahia.

plundering and razing the island as they left. The castle suffered severe damage during the earthquake of 1493 and was finally taken by the Turks when they occupied the island in 1522. Turks and Christians lived in it until 1821, but after the revolution the Turks removed the Christians, who then founded the settlements of Antimahia and Kardamaina.

The castle has an irregular, four-sided ground plan and the main entrance is in the north-west. The central gateway contains two entrances, one in the semicircular bastion and the other into the courtyard of the fort. It should be noted here that the semicircular bastion constitutes a later, 16th century addition. Set into the wall above the opening of the internal entrance is **the coat of arms of the Master D'Aubusson**, with the title of Cardinal and dated 1494, when repairs

The little chapel of Ayios Nikolaos inside the castle of Antimahia.

to damage caused by the earthquake of 1493 were completed. Immediately above the coat of arms there are three brackets which were intended to support the gallery with the well-known 'scalders' to keep the enemy at distance.

The size of the castle is evidence that there was a settlement inside it and that it also served as a place of refuge for people from other areas at times of danger. Leaving the castle and proceeding at first south and then east we come to the single-aisled

Frescoes from the little chapel of Ayios Nikolaos.

little Chapel of **Ayios Nikolaos**. There is a slab set into the wall above the entrance which bears the coat of arms of the Master Carretto (1513-21) in the above left-hand section, as well as the coat of arms of the

Order and the date 1520. It is probable that this church constituted part of a complex belonging to the Knights and that the slab is not in its original place, but had been brought there from elsewhere. Inside the church there is a fresco decoration dating from the 15th- 16th centuries. A little way beyond is the church of **Ayia Paraskevi**, also single-aisled and with sharply arched vaulting. To the right of it is a ruined building which was probably part of the church complex. In the northern wall of this building the coats of arms of the Master D'Aubusson and the Order are set into the wall. The church is dated to the post-Byzantine period. We leave the castle and follow the main road in a south-easterly direction. At a distance of 2.5 kilometres further on

The church of Ayia Paraskevi at Kardamaina.

The cosmopolitan beach of Kardamaina.

is the seaside village of **Kardamaina** which, with its wonderful sandy beach measuring 6 kilometres in length, has developed into a bustling resort with numerous tourist facilities and mainly vibrant night life. During the summer months there is a steamer connection from here to the island

The church of Ayia Paraskevi inside the castle of Antimahia.

Part of the archaeological site of Alasarna.

The picturesque beach path from Mastihari to the early Christian basilica.

of Nisyros, which lies opposite. Visit the majestic church of **Ayia Paraskevi** and look for traces of ancient **Alasarna** or Alasarni, parts of which (dating from various periods) have been discovered exactly beneath modern Kardamaina. During antiquity, Alasarna was the centre of the 'deme' of the Alasarnites. Earlier excavations brought to light a Roman theatre, while modern, systematic research since 1985 by the University of Athens, on a piece of ground exactly below the ancient acropolis and near to the theatre, has revealed important buildings of the Hellenistic period, as well as an extensive settlement of the late Roman and early Christian eras. In particular, a building of monumental dimensions (building A) with luxurious marble constructional elements dating from the 2nd century BC has been brought to light. Although it was originally identified as the temple of Apollo,

The site of the early Christian basilica at Mastihari is strewn with architectural fragments.

Clumps of sea-cedars at Mastihari.

researchers now believe that its designation as a religious structure is problematic, because of the absence of a stepped podium. A building discovered to the east of it (building B) has been interpreted as an altar, while in the north of the site excavation has revealed a building of monumental dimensions (8.24 x 15.43 metres, building C), filled inside with numerous pieces of architectural material. This building was almost certainly of a religious nature and has recently been identified as the temple of Apollo; it dates from the 3rd century BC. In the upper excavated layers of the same site, above the ancient buildings, houses have been discovered, some of which had two floors and storage cellars. These houses, along with the extensive burial complex which was found to the south-west of the site of the sanctuary, belonged to the early Christian settlement. Within the village of Kardamaina, on 28th October Street, there are the architectural remains of an early Christian basilica which was tripartite, wooden roofed, and had a narthex on the western side. West of the narthex there was a baptistery with a built,

The sandy beach at Mastihari.

cruciform font in the centre of it. The basilica is dated to the 5th century AD, and must have been destroyed around 553/4.

From Kardamaina we return to Antimahia and from there take the road to **Mastihari** (5 kms), the little seaport of Antimahia on the north coast of the island. On the way we come to the little church of Ayios Yeorgios, which has pieces of ancient architecture incorporated into its walls. Mastihari, offering a daily ferry connection to the island of Kalymnos which lies opposite, is a seaside village with a long, level beach of white sand in front of it. There is great tourist development here, and every type of modern facility. The **early Christian basilica of Ayios Yannis** in the south-west of the village is worth a visit; the way to it, along the pedestrian route which runs the length of the beach of Mastihari and then the narrow path which runs parallel to the shore, is one of great interest. After about 2 kilometres, passing amidst white sands and dunes with white lilies and pine trees which fill the area, our eyes drawn always to the sea, we come to the ruins of the early Christian basilica. It had a wooden roof and was divided into three aisles by means of pillars, with a narthex in the west. There was a baptistery in the north-east, rectangular in plan and with a polychrome mosaic on the floor. The basilica dates from the 5th century AD and was probably destroyed in the mid-6th century.

Kos - Ayios Stefanos -Kamari - Kefalos - Limionas - Ayios Yannis

The purpose of our last excursion is to get to know the south-west tip of the island. We begin from Kos, following the main arterial road in a south-westerly direction. After passing through Zipari, Linopotis and Antimahia and beyond the airport, we come to Plaka (27 kms). This is a magical, pine-covered locality where there is gurgling water, beautifully suited to a rest and a picnic. **The bay of Kefalos** with its sandy beaches opens out below us; there is strong tourist development here. Proceeding down towards the bay, little dirt tracks as well as some asphalt roads off to the left of the central road lead to wonderful, well-organised beaches such as Chrysi Akti, **Langades**, **Paradisos** and the beach of Ayios Stefanos, ideal for bathing and sea sports. At a distance of 36 kilometres along our route, immediately beyond the narrowest part of the island, we turn left towards the beach of **Ayios Stefanos**, in order to visit the early Christian basilica of the same name. The basilica is located right next to the sea, on a small, rocky peninsula on the eastern tip of the bay of Kefalos. In reality, it is a complex of two basilicas, one in the north and one in the south, which were discovered during excavations by L. Laurenzi in 1928. The south basilica had a wooden roof and two series of capitals separated its three aisles, of which the middle one formed a semicircular apse in the east. To the west of it was a narthex and in front of that, an atrium. The north basilica, exactly to the north of the latter, also had a wooden roof and was divided into three aisles with a series of alternating pillars and pilasters. The middle aisle also terminated in an apse to the east. A baptistery with a small dome in the middle and a cruciform font was situated to the east of the north basilica. Both

The rocky little island of Kastri on the Bay of Kefalos.

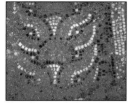

Part of a mosaic from Ayios Stefanos.

'Paradise' beach.

The beach of Ayios Stefanos, below the complex belonging to the famous hotel chain of Club Med.

basilicas are decorated with mosaic floors of excellent workmanship, depicting geometric designs and birds. Unfortunately however, the greater part of them is covered for protection and only small parts are visible. Only two of the marble and granite pillars have been reconstructed and are in their original position. The basilicas date from the 5th century AD and their destruction has been ascribed to the 6th century. In front of this complex, in the bay of Kefalos, there is the rocky little island called **Kastri**. ON the eastern edge of the bay, after Ayios Stefanos, there are the remains of another early Christian basilica, known as **'the Little Basilica of Kefalos'** where parts

Part of a mosaic from the 'little basilica' of Kefalos.

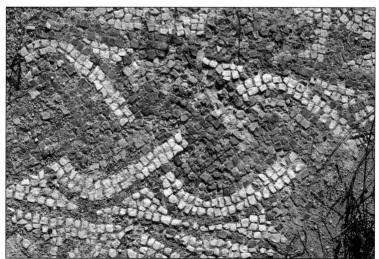

of mosaic floors with geometric designs can be seen. The basilica was brought to light by H. Balducci in 1935. The discovery of the basilicas mentioned above, and of one more at Kamari, all situated within the bay of Kefalos, justifiably led to questions about the Early Christian settlement to which they would have belonged. Archaeological excavations over the last decade have revealed that this settlement would have been a coastal one, spread over the length of the beach. Although investigations have only been sporadic and carried out in locations where the position of the present village permits excavation, the pieces of the puzzle relating to the early Christian settlement are gradually falling into place, revealing an older settlement with streets, a drainage system, and a number of private houses with rooms, courtyards, storehouses, stairways and arches. It developed upon the site of a Roman one, and most probably also upon one dating from the Hellenistic period which belonged to the well-known 'deme' of the Isthmiotes. The period of its greatest prosperity is certainly connected with the use of the commercial

The early Christian basilica with the little island of Kastri in the background.

The early Christian basilica of Ayios Stefanos, one of the most important sights of Kos.

The beach at Kamari.

The castle of Kefalos.

harbour at Kefalos, dated to the 5th century AD; the end of the settlement is ascribed to the arrival of the Arabs in 654 AD. If we follow the coastal road in a westerly direction we come to **Kamari**. This picturesque fishing village with a wonderful sandy beach also has a marina at the western end where dozens of fishing boats and caiques are moored. We leave Kamari and drive up the hill to the village of Kefalos, about 1.5 kilometres to the north. The remains of the **Castle of Kefalos** rise up to the right of the road; this excellent, secure fortification protected the inhabitants of Kos when they were forced to flee here during the Turkish invasion of 1457. From here the road continues to ascend until we come to the eastern edge of the village, where only a small part of the fortification is preserved. As the extant parts seem to

A traditional café at Kefalos.

correspond to those of a very small castle, the opinion has been expressed that such a building once existed here and was connected with a larger fort which has not been preserved. The extant parts of the wall consist of both unhewn and rectangular stones and are not of great thickness; on the exterior they stand to the impressive height of 11.5 metres, while internally they exist at ground level. The central gate is unfortunately not preserved; it was probably situated further west, towards the area of the

modern village. This castle must have been built during the period of the Knights, since the first mention of it has been dated to 1420. There is evidence that it was abandoned by the Knights in 1505, but occupation within its walls must have continued throughout the 16th and 17th

The Windmill of Papavasili at Kefalos.

110

Παραδοσιακό σπίτι
Traditional hous

The unique beach at Theologos, on the southern tip of the island.

centuries. We leave the castle and continue towards the **village of Kefalos** on the south-west tip of Kos. This mountain village is the farthest from the city of Kos, at a distance of 40 kms; it lies at the foot of Mount Zini, on a plateau formed on top of a craggy hill with a panoramic view out over the bay. Kefalos is a large village with an important tourist infrastructure. Given the mountainous nature of the terrain plant cultivation is limited here, in contrast to animal-keeping and mining. It is worth visiting the **traditional house** in the village with its wonderful, representative examples of handwork and general exhibits relating to everyday life at the beginning of the 20th century. Visitors can marvel, too, at the famous **windmill of Papavasili** nearby, which dominates from its position on an area of raised ground in the village. Kefalos was the first capital of Kos in antiquity, when it was called Astypalaia, before the consolidation of the island settlements in 366 BC. Parts of the ancient city, such as the Hellenistic theatre and the podium of a temple (probably of Demeter), have been discovered in the place called Palatia, to the north of the modern village, on the road to the south-

west tip of the island. The famous statue of Demeter was discovered in the same area, as well as the huge head of Herakles which can be seen today in the Archaeological Museum of Kos. At the spot called Palatia it is worthwhile paying a visit to the church of **Panayia Palatiani**, which is believed to have been built on top of an older Doric temple which may have been dedicated to Demeter; ancient building materials were used in the construction of the church. Beyond Palatia, there is a crossroads which leads, on the right, to **Ayios Theologos**. A little diversion of about 3.5 kilometres is recommended here, to an isolated

place of great natural beauty beside the sea, with holm-oaks and white sand; afterwards, we can return to the main road and continue in a south-westerly direction. A little further on there is a turn-off to the left towards Mount Zini, where the famous **cave of Aspri Petra** is located. Here, speleological and archaeological investigations carried out in 1922 by the Italian archaeologists A. de la Seta and Doro Levi revealed important palaeontological material, dating

from the end of the Neolithic period, as well as finds from the Mycenaean, Geometric and Roman periods. Together with the name of Mount Zini, which is itself connected with the name 'Zeus', the finds indicate the existence of a peak sanctuary in the area. We now return to the main road and continue again in a south-westerly direction; 2.5 kilometres further on we come to the Monastery of Ayios

Panayia Palatiani, a little outside the village of Kefalos.

The Monastery of Ayios Yannis.

Yannis, a total of 6.5 kilometres from Kefalos. This picturesque monastery occupies an idyllic position with a panoramic view towards Kos and the islands which lie opposite. From here, a dirt road continues to the southernmost tip of the island, Cape Krikellos. Leaving this beautiful area now behind us, we return to Kefalos. From the middle of the village a little track leads northwards, after about 4 kilometres, to the little, picturesque natural harbour and tended anchorage of **Limionas**. Here, you can take a rest in the little café, taste fresh fish and enjoy the peacefulness of the place when the sun begins to set.

The little harbour at Limionas.

BIBLIOGRAPHY

ΑΝΔΡΙΩΤΑΚΗΣ, ΧΡΙΣΤΟΦΟΡΟΣ Ν., *Κως, η πατρίς του Ιπποκράτους: ιστορία, αρχαιότητες, τουρισμός.*

DUBOIS M., *De Co Insula*, Paris and Nancy, 1884.

KIAPOKAS M.S., *Hippocrates of Cos and the Hippocratic Oath*, Athens 1999.

ΚΟΝΤΟΓΙΑΝΝΗΣ, ΝΙΚΟΣ Δ., *Μεσαιωνικά κάστρα και οχυρώσεις της Κω*, 2002.

ΜΠΟΥΡΑΖΕΛΗΣ, ΚΩΣΤΑΣ, *Kos between Hellenism and Rome: studies on the political, institutional, and social history of Kos from ca. the middle second century B.C. until late antiquity*, 1950.

PATON W.R ET AL., *The Inscriptions of Cos*, Oxford, 1891 / New York 1990.

RAYET, *Mimoire sur tile de Cos*, Paris, 1876.

ROSS LUDWIG, REISEN NACH KOS, *Halikarnassos, Rhodos und der Insel Cypern*, Halle: C. A. Schmetschfe & Sohn, 1852.

ROSS LUDWIG, *Reisen auf den griechischen Inseln*, Stuttgart, 1840-1845.

ΣΑΒΟΡΙΑΝΑΚΗΣ ΠΑΝΑΓΙΩΤΗΣ, *Νησιώτικες κοινωνίες στο Αιγαίο πριν και μετά τις Οθωμανικές μεταρρυθμίσεις: η περίπτωση των Ελλήνων της Ρόδου και της Κώ (18ος-19ος αιώνας)*, 2000.

SHERWIN-WHITE, SUSAN M., *Ancient Cos: an historical study from the Dorian settlement to the imperial period*, 1978.

ΣΚΑΝΔΑΛΙΔΗΣ, ΜΙΧΑΛΗΣ ΕΥΣΤ., *Τοπωνυμικά και ονοματικά της νήσου Κω.*

ΤΣΙΡΠΑΝΛΗΣ ΖΑΧΑΡΙΑΣ, *Η Ρόδος και οι Νότιες Σποράδες στα χρόνια των Ιωαννιτών Ιπποτών, 14ος-16ος αιώνες*, Ρόδος 1991.

ΖΑΡΡΑΦΤΗΣ ΙΑΚΩΒΟΣ Ε., *Το Ασκληπιείον της Κω : ήτοι περιγραφή του ανακαλυφθέντος αρχαίου ασκληπιείου της Κω και των σχετικών αυτού*, Εν Αθήναις 1912.

ΖΑΡΡΑΦΤΗΣ ΙΑΚΩΒΟΣ Ε., *Κώϊα: ήτοι Επτά τεύχη περιγράφοντα τα της Κω μετά του χάρτου αυτής*, Εν Κω 1921.

ΖΑΡΡΑΦΤΗΣ ΙΑΚΩΒΟΣ Ε., *Κωΐων: Ιστορία της Κω από των αρχαιοτάτων μέχρις ημών*, Κως Τύποις Ν. Ι. Νικολαΐδου 1922.

ΙΣΤΟΡΙΑ, ΤΕΧΝΗ, ΑΡΧΑΙΟΛΟΓΙΑ ΤΗΣ ΚΩ: Α΄ ΔΙΕΘΝΕΣ ΕΠΙΣΤΗΜΟΝΙΚΟ ΣΥΝΕΔΡΙΟ, Κως, 2-4 Μαΐου 1997.

ΧΑΤΖΗΒΑΣΙΛΕΙΟΥ ΒΑΣΙΛΗΣ, *Ιστορία της νήσου Κω*, 1990.

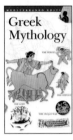

Greek Mythology
GREEK | ENGLISH | FRENCH | GERMAN |
DUTCH | SWEDISH | RUSSIAN

Orchids *Crete & Dodekanese*
GREEK | ENGLISH | GERMAN

Olive *Oil Way of long life*
ENGLISH | FRENCH | GERMAN |
DUTCH |SWEDISH | RUSSIAN

Athens
GREEK | ENGLISH

Kos *the island & the city*
GREEK | ENGLISH | GERMAN

Arkadi *The historic monastery*
GREEK | ENGLISH | FRENCH |
GERMAN | DUTCH | RUSSIAN

Rethymno, *The soul of Crete*
GREEK | ENGLISH | FRENCH |
GERMAN | SWEDISH

Chania *The City & The Prefecture*
GREEK | ENGLISH | FRENCH |
GERMAN | SWEDISH

Phaestos - Ayia Triada
GREEK | ENGLISH |
FRENCH | GERMAN

Fortezza *The Fortress of Rethymno*
GREEK | ENGLISH | GERMAN